Astrology & Numerology:

The Power Of Birthdays, Numbers, Stars & Their Secrets to Success, Wealth, Relationships, Fortune Telling & Happiness Revealed

© **Copyright 2019 by Sofia Visconti - All rights reserved.**

This document is geared towards providing exact and reliable information in regards to the topic and issue covered. The publication is sold with the idea that the publisher is not required to render accounting, officially permitted or otherwise qualified services. If advice is necessary, legal or professional, a practiced individual in the profession should be ordered.

From a Declaration of Principles which was accepted and approved equally by a Committee of the American Bar Association and a Committee of Publishers and Associations.

In no way is it legal to reproduce, duplicate, or transmit any part of this document in either electronic means or in printed format. Recording of this publication is strictly prohibited, and any storage of this document is not allowed unless with written permission from the publisher. All rights reserved.

The information provided herein is stated to be truthful and consistent, in that any liability, in terms of inattention or otherwise, by any usage or abuse of any policies, processes, or directions contained within is the solitary and utter responsibility of the recipient reader. Under no circumstances will any legal responsibility or blame be held against the publisher for any reparation, damages, or monetary loss due to the information herein, either directly or indirectly.

Respective authors own all copyrights not held by the publisher.

The information herein is offered for informational purposes solely and is universal as so. The presentation of the information is without a contract or any type of guarantee assurance.

The trademarks that are used are without any consent, and the publication of the trademark is without permission or backing by the trademark owner. All trademarks and brands within this book are for clarifying purposes only and are owned by the owners themselves, not affiliated with this document.

A SPIRITUAL START!

Start your week with gratitude, joy, inspiration, and love.

Healing, motivation, inspiration and guidance straight to your inbox every week!

FIND OUT MORE

Astrology:

Unlock The Secrets Of Your Life & Know Your Destiny Through The Stars

Contents

Introduction

Chapter One

Astrology: How does it work?
    The purpose of astrology
    Types of Astrology
    The importance of the planets in astrology

Chapter Two

All about Horoscope and Zodiac signs
    The Four Zodiac Elements
    The 12 Zodiac Signs
    Which horoscope are you compatible with?

Chapter Three

Understanding Relationships
    Houses
    Your Best Days for Romance & Friendships
    How to Bring Positive Energy To Your Relationships
    Why Are You Struggling With Relationships?

Chapter Four

Astrology & Your Finances

Chapter Five

Revealing Your Positive & Negative Personality Traits

Chapter Six

How To Take Control of Your Life Path & Purpose
    Achieve Emotional Stability
    Change Your Thinking

    Compartmentalize Your Relationships
    Avoid Distracting Negative Influences
    Meditation
    Be Intentional About Everything
    Be True to Yourself

Chapter Seven

What's Next In Your Life?
    Strengthen Your Inner Voice (Instinct)
    Tool for Self-Awareness/Discovery
    Build Compassion Towards Others
    Practical Guide Into Your Strengths & Weaknesses
    Useful for Career Guidance
    Be Prepared For Tough Times
    Insight Into The Future

Conclusion

Introduction

Astrology!

The word above can be a fascinating one for individuals because it has a myriad of meanings, think about this for a second, what picture forms in your mind when you think about the words Astrology? Do you think about your birthday? Or your love life? Do you cast your thoughts back to the time you felt like certain things happened to you because of your astrological sign?

Everything you think about astrology is somewhat part of the process as there are several layers to the idea. To explain it in simpler terms, you cannot have a complete conversation about life, finances, relationships, personality, etc. without considering the impact of astrology.

This book was carefully put together to help you gain access to the most detailed aspects and concepts about horoscope such that when you finish reading, you will be empowered with information that will help you make the right decisions and live a purposeful life.

If you embarked on a road trip before now, you would agree that one of the most exciting things about such a trip is the numerous stops you get to make with your travel buddies, and it is the same with this book. We are on a journey to unraveling essential information on astrology, yet all the information we seek are not embedded in a single chapter.

We will be making some stops so we can fully integrate every part of your life into the discourse. We will talk about the connection between astrology and your life in the most detailed way such that the application of knowledge gained will come naturally to you.

Are there moments in your life when you felt like you were no longer in control of what was going on or what was going to happen next? Well maybe you need to understand the fact that there is something higher than the physical realm and if you can fully grasp that idea you will not only be in control of your life you will also be able to avoid negative influences that distract you from your life's purpose.

Are you ready to get started on this trip? We will commence with a foundational chapter that encapsulates the main ideas of our subject matter: what is astrology, and how does it work?

Do enjoy the read!

Chapter One
Astrology: How does it work?

Astrology is referred to as the study of the influence of distinct cosmic objects over human lives. These astronomical objects are usually the stars, sun, moon and planets as they play a crucial role in shaping people's personality, romantic relationships, economic fortune and everything else about their existence.

Someone once said that "Life is what we make it", while this statement may hold sway when considering the impact of our personal choices and decisions, we cannot ignore the fact that astrology is a major determining factor as well.

Everything in the universes is connected and is in relationship with one another; we all know this through the connection between the rain that falls from the sky and the plants that grow bountifully because of it, everything is connected. Astrology is the correlation between heavenly bodies and the events that happen on earth.

Astrologers combine their scientific knowledge about the cosmos with other aspects such as intuition and man's psychological nature to create meaning out of events. Astrology also works with energy patterns while being focused on relationships, cycles and patterns that open doors and an understanding into our true psychological nature.

With astrology we go beyond the surface-level on what we are doing to ask the most fundamental question which is "Why are we doing what we are doing?" this type of understanding leads to self-acceptance, increased compassion and a sense of meaning in life while embracing the inspiration to evolve with purpose.

As you can already tell from this brief introduction thus far, astrology is an interesting topic to discuss because it makes you feel like you are looking in a mirror, only this time you don't get to see what you "Want" to know, you get to see who you are in the light of your connection with the universe.

Most people only think about their "Sign" when the word astrology is mentioned, they are referring to one of the 12 zodiac constellations, of course, your zodiac sign is a massive part of the discourse, but it isn't the heart of it. To understand astrology, you should be willing to open your heart to the universe and strive to know how it works.

Astrology is a mix of beliefs or practices that are described as scientific yet factual; it presents divine information about the affairs of human beings and their terrestrial events through the study of movements or positions of celestial objects.

Astrology also Maps the heavens at the moment of your birth and with that map any skilled astrologer can read the potentials of your life. OBSERVATION and EXPERIENCE are two striking words that remain relevant through the years when discussing astrology because the astrologers rely on what they observe about your birth map and the experience they gained through the years reading the maps of others.

Over thousands of years, we have discovered that the patterns we see in the night sky are a true reflection of the affairs in the earth or the potential they hold. This also means that there are varying mediums through which these patterns can be unearthed.

From divination to prophecy, fortune telling and omens, astrology has birthed several mediums such that interpretation is no longer streamlined to one pattern, and all of these contributes to making the discourse an exciting one.

So now you are wondering, if astrology is real why is your horoscope at the back of the newspaper not accurate? Well you should understand that what you read in the newspaper is not as comprehensive as you expect it to be as it is simply based on one feature, the sign the sun was in when you were born.

For a more holistic analysis, you would need to get your reading from your accurate horoscope which is not only based on the sun but at least on nine of the other celestial bodies. An account of where you were born on earth, the time and where you are sitting at the moment is also crucial.

Also, the date, time and location of your birth with your current position will be necessary to drawing and reading the natal map and your horoscope. Now you know why you may not be getting what you seek in the newspaper because the astrologers do not have these personalised details of everyone that reads the paper. You will learn more about zodiac signs in the next chapter and how all of these are connected to your readings.

The study of astrology dates back to thousands of years, and it all began with man's realization that we are not the sole architect of our fortunes or misfortunes. We do have a measure of control over our lives, but if we are going to be very successful, we must become aware of the impact of astrology in the fabrics of our existence.

Astrology isn't restricted to particular world culture; neither does it have much more significance in one part of the world than another. The reason you may feel like some sects of people have dominion over it is because they actively practice and search for more depth with astrology than others. Regardless of the extent of practice or realization of its importance, one thing is for sure, astrology is a pivotal part of our lives.

In its broader sense, astrology is about the search for meaning in the sky. In the earlier days, humans used signs for the sky to predict seasonal changes and the influence of the moon on their communal calendar. This sky search represented the earliest attempts by human beings to create and sustain the bond between their world and the celestial space.

More so, astrology is also a method through which mundane events can be predicted based on the "Special" relationship that exists between individual celestial bodies and their motions. This unique relationship is one of the reasons why some zodiac signs are compatible (concerning relationships), and some others are incompatible.

Despite the success recorded with astrology, it had ancient objections, and even in modern times some people still argue about the influence of astrology because for them it doesn't make sense to look at the universe for answers.

But think about this, who or what else do we turn to for answers other than the universe? When babies are born, they remain attached to their mothers not just at the initial birth stage but all throughout their lives and this mother-child relationship is what we have with the universe.

Astrology becomes the bridge through which we can connect with the universe to get answers to several questions we may have. In the course of reading this book, you will be amazed at the level of influence astrological concepts have over your life and how you can make better decisions when you understand it in its entirety.

The fact that most horoscope predictions are patterned after the signs following your birth chart further validates the authenticity of astrology in your life. But we are not going to dedicate time towards trying to "Convince" you that this is a path worth taking, after all, regardless of your beliefs in rainbows, they still show up after the rain!

Which means that even if you don't have as much faith in astrology, it doesn't change the fact that things are aligning for you based on the celestial factors and whenever you come to the knowledge of this truth (as you would through this book) you will be empowered to utilize it for your good.

Our souls speak to us all the time, not with mere words but with symbols and the language of images but you will need a channel through which you can grasp the meaning of what is being said, this is where astrology comes in. With astrology, you have the proven techniques for receiving the messages and concepts from the universe into your conscious mind.

While some people believe that the planets cause certain events, feelings and circumstances to happen, with astrology we get to see that the planet only reflects the energy that surrounds us while providing insight into how we can use the power to create better relationships, make sound financial choices and live a happier life.

But none of these explicitly talks about the primary purpose of astrology, of course, we already know what we can use it for but what was the original intention? Are we still in line with what works? Are there other ideas on how astrology works?

The purpose of astrology
The initial goal of astrology is multi-faceted; on the one hand, it is meant to be an avenue for individuals to get information on the course of their life. On the other hand, it presents an opportunity for people to gain access to the seasons of the world and how they affect productivity with

aspects such as agriculture (this was the earliest purpose in earlier times).

However, in today's world the purpose of astrology has taken much more specific pathways, from relationships to finance, marriage and even job opportunities, people now seem to have better control of their lives due to the influence of astrology.

There is also the cathartic purpose of astrology, which determines if the particular moment is astrological right for the success of a course of action. An individual can choose to act in a way that will be favorable to him or her to avoid future predicaments and problems.

The purpose of interrogatory astrology is to provide answers to the questions a person may have based on the situation of the heavens at a peculiar time. This purposeful use of astrology is closer to divination as the individual will want to ascertain how the heavens will either support or decline or action.

But overall, astrology is meant to help you work closely with the universe, so your actions are in alignment with what the universe holds for you. Before gaining consciousness of astrology, you probably walked without direction while "Hoping" that the world will fall in line, but this is a problematic thought process.

We don't have to hope that the universe falls in, line because that will mean we are making plans outside of what the universe has planned for us. The issue is that regardless of your intentions, including the universe or not, what is meant to happen based on your astrological assessment will still occur.

So the best bet will be for you to take the universe on this ride with you by looking out for what it is saying and then making decisions based on what you receive from the energy around you.

Types of Astrology

As it is with the different purposes of astrology, there are also types of astrology, and some of them include:

1. *Horoscope Astrology*

This astrology studies a person's current experiences with the astrologer looking at the chart that focuses on where the planets are on a particular day.

At the time of birth this becomes your natal chart, but the planets don't stop moving, and as they move through the heavens the concepts between them and your initial natal planet position will show the events that will happen in your life.

With horoscope astrology you will also get an insight into the day-to-day activities you may encounter which explains why some people say they don't want to go out on certain days because their "Horoscope" tells them not to.

2. *Horary astrology*

Horary astrology is a unique form of astrology focused on helping you get astrological answers quickly. There are no activities or calendars involved neither do you have to sit under the open sky contemplating the stars.

Horary astrology is also about the theory of synchronicity and the causality of time, which makes it a predictive form of astrology. When the astrologer is asked a question, he draws a chart as soon as he hears the question.

With the drawing, the astrologer gets the answer to the question and the puzzle (whatever it is, is resolved).

3. Synastry astrology

With astrology, people are not only concerned about what they can do or how it affects their life but how it also relates to other people. So synastry astrology is the study of how people relate with each other. You can relate one natal chart with another and study how the planets intermingle with one another.

Synastry astrology is mostly used for romantic readings that have to do with questions such as "Is this person and I a good match?", "Will this relationship work with this person?" etc.

This astrology also relates to families and the kind of relationship you have with your colleagues at your workplace.

4. Natal astrology

There is a lot of connection between astrology and the times we were born; this is the major preoccupation with natal astrology. This form of astrology seeks to use the moment you were born to draw a map of the heavens, which is referred to as a natal chart that shows the potential of your life.

Natal astrology also makes it easier for us to learn more about our personalities, the unique talents we have and the possibilities these ideas can bring to our lives. To express it in simpler terms, natal astrology is a person's guide or map of their life.

5. Zodiac astrology

Zodiac astrology is the most popular type of astrology, even those who are not very knowledgeable on things about astrology know zodiac (kids inclusive). At some point in your life you may have sat with your friends to discuss each other's horoscope and laughed off what you discovered.

Well, each of the planets influences one of the zodiac stars (which are 12 in total, the next chapter will focus more on this). Each of the zodiac stars is controlled by one planet as the movement of the planet gives insight into what the future holds the signs (Leo, Libra, etc.).

There is a lot of information on zodiac signs online and offline; people like to talk about the compatibility with signs, fortune, luck and how different people belong to different zodiac signs with the degree of success they bring to people's lives.

The extent of belief you choose to show towards zodiac signs is up to you, but for this foundational chapter, it is crucial that you become acquainted with this type of astrology because it is a recurring idea you will encounter in later parts of this book.

6. Fixed stars astrology

The galaxy can be a bit mysterious, and although scientist is always working on solving the mystery, it remains puzzling. Most of the time, astrology focuses on celestial concepts, the aspects that make up the solar system, but there is a level beyond this.

The level entails the inclusion of stars that existed long before we came along. The fixed stars astrology tries to explore the fact that things are not only understood by the mind alone but by those who take the time to contemplate the universe and what lies ahead of it.

The stars we concentrate on with this type of astrology does not move around the sun, the sun is not in the middle of their universe, and they are fixed in a particular position without changing.

The study of these fixed stars birthed this branch of astrology yet it cannot be done in isolation. Fixed stars astrology must be done about the planets, the bodies around it and other factors that affect it.

There is a need to build a relationship and strike a connection between all of these concepts to give the astrologer a complete picture of what is being sought after. So the unmoving stars are the objects of contemplation and study but they are studied with other planets as well.

7. Medical Astrology

If you want to consider medical astrology you must be very good with biology, go back and review the basics to refresh your memory if you've forgotten. You will need to know all about the different parts of the body with medical astrology, how the body parts are connected, and how they come together to act as a whole system.

The body parts are doing great on their own, but when they work together, we know it's like magic, and the coordination between them is crucial for good health and well-being.

Each part of the body has its associated symbols or astrological sign; it has also been said that different planets have the rule over the various body organs thus it is often complicating deciding on the planet that controls a part of the body.

This is where medical astrology comes into play; it is the study of the relationship between the organs of the body, its symbols, and how they aid better life experiences for an individual.

8. Karmic astrology

Karmic astrology is not as popular or well-known as the other types, but it is an exciting concept. Karmic is all about having belief in the idea of reincarnation, which is a massive leap of faith as not many people are willing to take about reincarnation.

Some reincarnation goes against certain beliefs and science, but there is no harm done when studying it to learn more about astrology, it then becomes your choice to either believe it or not.

Amongst all the types of astrology, this one tends to push reality the most as it celebrates the idea that you are born in a different form before now and you will remain that way for years to come.

Life is a continually evolving circle, and though we may not when we started with the ring or when it will end, with karmic astrology, you gain insight into your "Past" life and its present reality.

The people who find karmic astrology fascinating are those who are always in search of how life started and how the circle is created. Such persons are drawn to karmic astrology because they believe that it can provide answers regarding the hunt for more detailed facts about life.

Facts, stories and every other idea that helps a person understand the concept of their past life and they're present one are all presented with the karmic astrology.
Sometimes we become so engrossed in our determination to seek astrological answers that we become oblivious of what is right and wrong, what is up to us to decide and what is not. Don't get carried away in your search for a "Sign" even when there aren't any at a time, don't become consumed with the movement of the stars and the planets that you fail to recognize the role you play in developing your life beyond astrological predictions.

It is crucial that you know how to strike a balance with everything.

Some people wait for a sign before taking a job or starting a relationship with a great person, in fact for some others they spend a large part of their adult life just waiting for the "Stars to align", while it is great to watch the stars don't do it excessively.

Yes, you should know as much as you can about astrology, you are doing a great job reading this book but do not become obsessed over it by allowing it to run your life. Don't stay back at home because you feel it's a "Bad" day to go to work. The general purposes of astrology is give you control of your life and not to intimidate you into living a frightful life.

The importance of the planets in astrology

1.   The Sun
There are two very bright objects we consider in the sky with astrology, and there are the Sun and the moon. The Sun is the most brilliant of both, and it represents fiery energy that is active, masculine, and very strong.

The Sun is also a sign placement for the ego and the way a person expresses him/herself. Through the Sun, we gain insight into the concept of self-expression with astrology as those under this planet draw their creativity and vibrant leadership style from its energy.

The Sun in astrology also represents your SOUL; it is your power and strength to walk through life winning even in the face of dire challenges. So when you think about the Sun in astrology also think about the person's inner strength.

Although in the scientific world, the Sun is not considered a planet, in astrology, it is a planet. It represents your father, masculinity, which explains the reason why you wouldn't have a good relationship with your father. Not having a good relationship with your father only happens when the Sun is placed wrongly on your horoscope.

This situation with your father also means that your vitality and inner willpower weakens. But when the Sun placed in your horoscope, then it means you will blossom in your career. You will have the willpower to conquer whatever comes your way.

2. The Moon

The moon represents your personality, emotions, mental projections, and the way you think. Some people erroneously believe that it is the sun sigh that is responsible for their character, but that isn't true.

The moon sign determines how you are going to think and behave in certain situations. Moon also symbolizes mother (femininity), which means that if your moon is not well placed, you might not have a good relationship with your mother. You might also be in constant collision with your mum.

With a well-placed moon, you can handle a lot of stress and handle situations in a better way. The moon is also a representation of your unconscious habits, your moods, gut feeling, and the capacity you build to nurture anything (relationships, career, etc.).

3. Mercury

Mercury is the fastest moving planet that represents the mind and its intellect. Mercury is also associated with communication, based on the in-flow and out-flow levels that speak of how you communicate with yourself and others.

In classical Roman Mythology, Mercury was known as a messenger because he was always very swift and fast. In today's world, the same features apply to the signs ruled by Mercury.

So in astrology, Mercury represents rationality, thinking patterns, and reasoning. Mercury can be inconsistent and curious but rules over the day-to-day expressions in a relationship.

Mercury could also be said to be the neutral planet that serves as the glue, holding everything for two or more individuals together. Mercury also symbolizes being practical and scientific, with curiosity being a significant factor for those who have Mercury in their fourth house.

4. Venus

Venus represents emotions such as feelings of love, appreciation for beauty, and a desire for harmony. If Venus placed in a person's 7th house, then it could mean that the individual is ready for a successful relationship that could lead to marriage.

Venus is a significant indicator of luxury, convenience, and value for material things. This love for material things and other people means that the two distinct attributes of Venus cut across the material level and the interpersonal level.

On the material level, it is all about WHAT we value, houses? Cars? Art? Etc. while on the interpersonal level it is all about WHO we value, our spouses? Friends? Etc.

Those who are ruled by this planet have a certain charisma about them that enables them to draw people into their circle. Making others feel comfortable is one of the things that makes Venus a very peculiar planet. This planet attracts, making it a unique world when considering astrological connections.

Within birth charts, Venus also governs courtship and the commitment to the process of being in love with an individual which speaks of its true nature as the planet that rules love.

5. Mars

Mars is known as the "Red Planet," and it represents your physical and mental fighting strength and the desire to take action. There is anger in the individual who has Mars poorly placed in his horoscope. Mars is also known for its aggressive instincts and drive.

A well placed Mars will translate into strength for the individual, yes he/she can get angry but expresses it in a very dignified manner. Mars also symbolizes male friends and brothers because it is masculine energy (but this doesn't include your father because the Sun symbolizes him)

Mars also symbolizes strength when placed in an individual's horoscope. You will find that such persons can go through a lot of defeat in life and get back on top.

Their anger can also be channeled positively into well-meaning projects that will help those mistreated. Most boxers, athletes and fighters have a well-placed Mars in their horoscope because they are born hunters.

Mars also represents those who are risk takers as evident in its rule "Aries". Mars is that planet that gets you up and going daily; it helps you become expressive with your anger, empowers you to embrace your sex drive and the desire to give into a sexual relationship.

Depending on when you were born, if Mars were reverting, you would direct your energy internally and do your best to avoid confrontation. On the flip side, if Mars was unchanging at the time of your birth, you will be all about actions and going for what you want because you are your priority.

6. Jupiter

Sagittarius is the sign rules for this planet, and it is all about growth. Jupiter guides your ethics and philosophy about life; it concentrates on when you are either lucky, abundant, cautious, and where you want to learn with how you can benefit from the knowledge gained about life.

Jupiter is a lucky charm that tends to expand whatever it touches; it shows what you do on a large scale and where you receive financial benefits.

Jupiter also displays the extent of your generosity towards others while being on the search for truth at all times. If your chart has the Jupiter sign, then you will be a person who loves to make the planet perfect for governed laws and a better place for people to live.

Jupiter is also all about religion, philosophy and education. If this planet was reverting when a person was born, then the individual will be quite philosophical. If Jupiter were stagnant at the person's birth, he/she would have strong opinions and well-grounded principles.

7. **Saturn**
Capricorns are under this planet, and it is all about achievement!
Saturn tends to describe your ambition in life with your major life lessons and the feelings of inadequacy. This planet is about restrictions, boundaries, limitations, safety and practicability.

If you find this planet on your chart, then you are most likely a hardworking fellow who gets what he/she deserves. Saturn is the planet that oversees your business, wealth and career.

Sometimes even if its placement in your chart doesn't affect your career directly, it will show that you are someone who wants to be an achiever and a person who wants to be known for the work they execute excellently.

If Saturn was inverse at your birth time, you will be proactive with your success and be responsible for your achievements and failures. If Saturn was stagnant when you were born, then you are probably a goal-oriented individual who is disciplined, focused on the big picture and determined to succeed at all cost.

6. Uranus

This planet represents the creative imagination of a person as well as his/her intuition with talent and psychology. For Uranus, it is all about seeing things in a better perspective, being an advocate for change and an encourager for rebellion.

This planet prepares the person for changes in life and strengthens their beliefs with regards to their set goals and the things they want to achieve in life. Uranus is also about eccentricity with the individual exhibiting unique characteristics that make him/her stand out.

Adventurous, friendly, and outgoing are some of the words that can be used to describe the person who is ruled by Uranus. The planet also influences the individual to absorb the spirit of the new age hence making them reformers and inventors.

7. Neptune

This planet affects people who become risk-takers and are always willing to take chances. One of the significant attributes of the people ruled by Neptune is their childlike faith and innocence which makes them get opportunities even when

For some people ruled by this planet, they feel a certain level of imbalance in their balanced and this attributed to the vast nature of Neptune's orbit. So, for example, a Libra individual used to being calm can suddenly become erratic when Neptune rules over his/her sign.

Those in the Neptune sign are described as dreamy. Their whimsical nature connected to mythology and the history of the planet. Unlike Venus, which focuses on self-love alone, Neptune is concerned with mutual love.

8. Pluto

This planet is about transforming the old aspects of self and coming into new experiences. To move forward with life as a person influenced by Pluto, you need to have an inner consciousness of the changing time and cultivate the resilience to move from the past into the future.

The fears that Pluto ruled sign carries are deeply rooted in the fact that they are easily attached to certain things and wouldn't want to let go. Pluto is the furthest of the planets and the smallest. But it has a lot of concentrated power hence the reason those under this planet hold an in-depth view of the world (they often delve into philosophy).

This chapter is a foundational one that seeks to provide insight into the fundamental concepts of astrology. What we have achieved with this section is to introduce you to vital keywords you will most likely encounter all through the book.

The next stop for us will be a chapter on the connection between horoscope and zodiac signs. If you probably knew anything at all about astrology as a discourse before now, it would be zodiac signs, so get ready to gain additional insight into what you know.

Chapter Two
All about Horoscope and Zodiac signs

This chapter is going to build on what we learned in the previous section as you will get to discover all the specific details about horoscopes and zodiac signs with a keen focus on how it relates to you. As mentioned in the previous chapter, the zodiac sign is one of the most popular ideas when discussing astrology with anyone.

Most people know more about the zodiac than anything else relating to astrology because they want to be connected with the idea that shows them what they look like and how they can do better with life.

There are 12 zodiac signs; each sign has got its strengths and weaknesses with its unique traits, attitudes, and desires. The signs also have peculiar features that relate to how individuals behave towards other people. The analysis of the positions of the sun and moon on the ecliptic moment of birth gives us a glimpse of a person's character, preferences, fears, and flaws.

In this chapter, you will discover every detail you need about the zodiac signs, the character of your sun sign, its horoscope traits, your profile, history, myths and more excitedly your love compatibility.

Before getting to the zodiac signs, you should know that each of them belongs to the four elements (air, water, earth, and fire). The features are an essential type of energy that is present in each of us. With astrology, we can focus the energies on positive aspects of life and have a better appreciation of our traits.

The four zodiac elements help describe your unique personality as it is associated with astrological signs and has such an impressive effect on your character traits, emotions, and behavior.

The Four Zodiac Elements

Air signs
These signs are for rational, love, social communication, and relationship with other people. There are also for thinkers, intellectuals, people who are analytical and highly communicative. Such persons love philosophical discussions, good books, and social gatherings where they get to interact with like minds.

Those who are in the Air sign category also love giving good advice, and the zodiac signs under this element are Gemini, Aquarius, and Libra.

Fire signs
Fire signs are very temperamental; they are passionate and dynamic people who have a lot of energy. Yes, they get easily offended, but they also forgive easily as well. They are adventurous, very strong physically, and always inspiring to others.

Those who have the fire signs are also self-aware, intelligent, idealistic, and creative; they are always ready for action and Aries, Sagittarius and Leo are in this category.

Earth signs
Those in this category are grounded; they are conservatives and genuine people who can be emotional as well. They are also efficient people, loyal, and stable.

Sticking by people through difficult times is one of their strong suits, and the earth signs include Taurus, Virgo, and Capricorn.

Water signs
These are emotionally and ultra-sensitive people who are also highly intuitive, they tend to be mysterious but are lovers of intimacy and profound conversations. They always support those they love, and the water signs are Scorpio, Cancer, and Pisces.

The 12 Zodiac Signs

For each of the zodiac signs below, you will find the birth dates for easy identification of your sign (if you don't already know it).

Aquarius (January 20 – February 18)
Aquarius is a naturally shy and quiet individual, but he/she can also be very energetic. They are deep thinkers who are intellectual in nature with a love for helping others. They do not take sides when two persons are embroiled in conflict; hence, the reason they are trusted with conflict resolution.

They also have a deep need to be left alone and stay far away from everything even though they can adapt quickly to the energy around them. When they are not mentally stimulated, they tend to be bored and lack motivation. These are people who see possibilities in the world when others see a bleak future, and they tend to use their mind at every opportunity they get.

Aquarius is ruled by the planet Uranus as such they tend to be timid, abrupt and aggressive sometimes just like the planet. But they also have a visionary ability which makes it easier for them to predict future happenings thus the reason most of them know precisely what they should be doing five years to come

Uranus also gives them the ability to transform quickly, making it possible for them to be progressives, thinkers, and humanists. When they are in a group or a community, they feel good, which is why they always want to be surrounded by people.

One of the problems of the Aquarius born is the fact that they have a feeling of being constrained because of their desire for freedom and equality for all. They also come off as being insensitive persons who are cold at heart, but this is only a defense mechanism they use to avoid being open to intimacy to people they don't trust.

The Aquarius born needs to learn how to trust others while also getting better at being expressive with emotions in a healthy way. They also need to understand that when people disagree with them, it doesn't mean they are not liked.

The Aquarius person runs away from emotional expressions but is also fun to be with friends and is an excellent listener. Such an individual is original.

Pisces (February 19 – March 20)
These are friendly people who find themselves in the company of varying types of people, but regardless of where they are, they remain selfless. Pisces are always willing to help others without getting in return.

They are guided by the water sign as such, characterized by empathy and high emotional capacity. Their planet is Neptune, so this makes them highly intuitive than other people. They also have an artistic side hence the reason they are music lovers (their love for music manifests at an early age).

Pisces are generous individuals who are also compassionate towards the plight of people in need; they are faithful to their partners and friends and show an extreme level of care that others seek to emulate.

People born under these signs have an intuitive understanding of the life cycle, so they achieve a lot with their relationships. They are also known for their uncanny wisdom, thus being able to give good advice to people in stressful situations.

Due to the influence of the planet, Uranus on their lives, people born under this sign can take on the role of a martyr, which further bolsters the fact that they are selfless.

The people born under this sign are never judgmental, and they tend to forgive those who offend them quickly, in fact, they are the most tolerant of all the zodiac signs.

Pisces always have a desire to escape reality because they are easily trusting and get hurt; this makes them fearful and sad. They can be termed as "People who know it all" thus they are often criticized. Their past comes back to haunt them, making them have feelings of regret early in life.

Aries (March 21 –April 19)
This is the first zodiac sign, and by its position, it always marks the beginning of something tremendous yet turbulent. Personalities under this sign are consistently looking for ways to compete and wanting to be first with everything.

Aries is also one of the most active zodiac signs, and this is mostly attributed to the fact that its ruling planet is Mars, and it also belongs to the Fire sign just like Leo and Sagittarius.

Due to the influence of the sun on the sign, they have excellent organizational skills hence the reason when you meet an Aries he/she can get several things done all at once. When they become impatient, you will get to see their behavioral flaws.

The stronger personalities that are born under this sign have to fight to achieve their goals while embracing the idea of teamwork and togetherness, Aries and rulers and leaders over other heads, they are naturally brave and are not afraid of taking risks.

Aries also possess youthful looks and energy such that irrespective of their age they can still complete tasks. Aries is also courageous and optimistic when others are doubtful. Their enthusiasm can be contagious, making those they meet very comfortable around them.

Aries individuals can be short-tempered when they feel like they are not getting what they need, which can also make them impulsive and sometimes aggressive. They like comfortable clothes, physical challenges, and enjoy individual sports.

On the flip side, they do not like inactivity, nor do they tolerate delays. They believe in working with one's talents and take leadership roles seriously.

Taurus (April 20 – May 20)
These are well-grounded individuals who are also practical; they feel the urge to be surrounded by love and positivity at all times and love physical pleasures. People born under this sign love to enjoy the fruits of their labor, they also consider taste and touch as the most important senses.

They are stable conservatives making them the most reliable of all the zodiac signs as they are always ready to endure and maintain their choices until they attain personal satisfaction.

The sign for Taurus is Earth; these individuals can see things from a practical perspective, which is realistic as well. They also tend to make money easily while staying on a single project for many years until it is completed.

What so many other people see in them as stubbornness is commitment and their ability to finish a project they started. Taurus are excellent employees, the right partners, and supportive long-term friends who will stand by you through all the curveballs life throws at you.

Due to their connection with Earth, they tend to be overprotective. They are also materialistic sometimes with views about the world based on two things: money and wealth.

Taurus is connected to the planet Venus which happens to be the planet of love, creativity, beauty and attraction. These tender attributes makes the Taurus person a great cook, lover, artist and gardener. They are also loyal people who do not like spontaneous changes or criticism.

Regardless of how emotionally attached to a situation they can still talk with a practical tone and be the voice of reason in an unhealthy situation. Taurus individuals are uncompromising and possessive when they want to be.
They are also viewed as responsible people in society who are devoted to causes dear to their hearts. They are the reliable ones, friends, and family can count on at any time.

Gemini (May 21 – June 20)
Geminis express two varying personalities in one person, and you wouldn't be sure of the one you will face at any time. They can be very friendly, ready to have a good time, and quick-witted.

Geminis can be very playful one moment and suddenly become serious; this shows the presence of the dual personalities they embody. They have a huge fascination for the world, which makes them curious, but they never seem to have enough time to experience what they envision.

Gemini belongs to the Air signs while being ruled by Mercury, the planet that represents movement, communication, and writing. The people born under this sign tend to deal with a feeling of missing someone who should complete them, hence the reason they consistently search for friends, colleagues, and people to share a bond with.

The Gemini has a flexible open mind, which makes him/her very artistic. Their skills also make them shine in trade sectors and sports, they are versatile, fun loving and have an innate wish to experience all that is out there in the world.

They have a very inspiring character that isn't boring, and this is because they are affectionate, gentle, and can quickly adapt to any situation. Geminis have the ability to learn quickly while exchanging ideas with others swiftly; they can make personality switches within seconds to suit the peculiar situation.

They are also lovers of music, books, magazines and short trips around time. But Geminis can be inconsistent because of the dual personality situation, which also makes them nervous and indecisive.

Cancer (June 21 – July 22)
This is one of the most challenging of all the zodiac signs; they are intuitive yet sentimental, very emotional, but equally sensitive. Those under the Cancer sign care for their family genuinely, they have a thoughtful way of getting attached to people, and they are loyal individuals.

It is easy for a Cancer to empathize with other people's pain and suffering because they are guided by their emotions and heart. Although they could have a hard time blending into the world around them, this can be traced to their childhood experiences when they had a hard time coping with others.

They have a lot of mood swings, lack patience, and can use self-pity to manipulate others (which makes them appear selfish sometimes). They are always quick to help other people, ready to avoid conflict. When they are at peace with the choices they make in life, they will have a feeling of content while being surrounded by their family and loved ones.

Those under the Cancer sign love the thrill of having a loving family in a happy home, and they are patriots who will fight the cause of others even if they have to endanger their lives. Cancers are tenacious and highly imaginative individuals who can be persuasive.

They also tend to be insecure, hence the reason for their suspicion of everyone else, which leads to pessimism and moodiness. They like to relax near water, have a good meal, and enjoy hobbies at home.

Leo (July 23 – August 22)
Natural born leaders are under the Leo sign; they are an exciting group of people who are dramatic, self-confident, and creative. Leos can dominate any situation are difficult to resist; they can achieve whatever they set to do in any area so long they are committed to it.

Leos tend to have the "King of the Jungle" mentality, which makes them have so much faith in themselves. They are quite generous, loyal to others, and have many friends. Leos are also attractive, they fall under the Sun sign and are capable of bringing different groups of people together Leos can lead people towards a shared cause, and with their healthy sense of humor, they make collaborations easier, thus making the goals easily achievable.

The Leo sign belongs to the Fire element like Aries and Sagittarius, so they are warmhearted people who are in love with life, always having a good laugh and a good time. They can solve the most challenging problems using their minds and can get out of complicated situations.

Leos are always in search of self-awareness and the growth of their ego; they are also aware of their desires and the effect their personality has on others but can easily neglect the others in pursuit of their gain and status.
Most Leos have people who do not like them and want to pull them down, especially in workplaces and other competitive spaces, this because Leos have very intimidating success track records.

Leos are also warm-hearted when you get close to them, they can be cheerful, humorous, and they like admiration. But they dislike being ignored which could present them as being self-centered individuals.

Virgo (August 23 – September 22)
One thing you will notice about a Virgo is the fact that they pay attention to the tiniest details. They also have a deep sense of humanity making them one of the most careful individuals of all the signs. Virgos have a systematic pattern for life that makes them take charge of everything and leave nothing to fate, chance, or luck.

They can be very tender, yet their hearts may be closed off to the world, which can make them entirely misunderstood sign because they can express themselves, but they wouldn't accept their feelings as real.

They often feel like they are experiencing everything for the first time; their sign is the earth making them a perfect fit for Taurus and Capricorn. Virgos are influential leaders but are also conservative, well-organized, and like the practicality of life.

A Virgo likes to be organized; sometimes, even in a chaotic situation, they remain organized with strictly defined goals and dreams. They worry about missing out on any detail that could be too difficult to fix later on, and they can spend a significant amount of time obsessing over details.

These individuals can also be critical and too concerned about issues that other people do not care about. Mercury is Virgo's ruling planet, which is a representation of having a well-developed sense of speech, writing, and other forms of communication.

A lot of Virgos may want to pursue writing a career or a career in journalism because of their natural writing skills. They are also born with an innate desire to serve others, thus making them the perfect choice as caregivers who are on a mission to help others.

Virgos can be shy when in the presence of people they admire, but they are loyal, hardworking, kind, and analytical with what they do. They also tend to worry over everything else while being overly critical of themselves and others. They believe in the mantra "All work and no play" stressing on their addiction to work and being much focused.

Virgos like animals, books, food, and cleanliness but they also like to take center stage, which makes some people view them as being rude.

Libra (September 23 - October 22)
People born under the Libra sign are very peaceful, and they hate being alone. They are keen on partnerships, are fascinated by symmetry, balance, and always in chase of justice, fairness, and equality. Show me an activist who will not give up on his/her quest; you will see a Libra through and through.

Libra can do anything to avoid conflict even when they advocate for equality; they will instead take the peaceful approach. The sign for Libra is the Air; they are active intellectuals who go through constant mental stimuli while being inspired by good books.

Those born in the Libra sign also have a lot to say, but they must be careful about what they say when surrounded by people (they could get into trouble by saying the wrong thing to the wrong crowd).

They do not want a partner who makes them disregard their own opinions, and they are great lovers as well who like expensive, material things. They love to visit beautiful places and are lovers of fine art. A Libra can be fair-minded and social yet indecisive.

They also find it easy practicing self-pity on themselves when they feel they have been offended, and this can make them hold a grudge for a long time. Although very cooperative, Libras do not like to conform to the set norms, they don't like loudmouthed individuals, but they love to share with others.

Scorpio (October 23 – November 21)

These are very passionate individuals who are also assertive. They are entirely focused, determined, and decisive with the will to seek out the truth until they find it. A Scorpio is a great leader who is aware of situations and tries to use his/her resourcefulness to calm the waters.

Scorpio is also a water sign and lives for experiences and the expression of emotions. Yes, feelings are essential to the Scorpio, but they tend to manifest them differently than other water signs. The Scorpio can keep a secret (regardless of what it is).

The planet for transformation and regeneration is Pluto, and this is the ruling planet for Scorpio; hence, the reason for their calm and relaxed demeanor. They often have a mysterious appearance as people tend to say Scorpio-born individuals are fierce, but this because they understand the rules of the universe.

Some Scorpio looks older than their actual age, but they are also excellent leaders, dedicated to what they do. They hate dishonest behavior, and they can be extraordinarily jealous, but Scorpio needs to learn how to adapt to situations quickly.

Those born under this sign are brave, they have a lot of friends because they attract the right kind of people, and they are good friends to others (very supportive). They can build long-term friendships because they are honest (so there is little or no misunderstanding with their friends).

A Scorpio doesn't like it when someone else reveals a secret because they detest dishonesty and passive individuals. If you have a Scorpio in your corner, you have a true friend indeed. Sometimes a Scorpio can be branded as being stubborn, but this is also interpreted as bravery for some other persons.

Most striking about them is their resourceful nature, it is never a dull or mediocre moment with a Scorpio, they always know how to get things done

Sagittarius (November 22 – December 21)
The individuals under this sign are powerful communicators; they are so good at expressing themselves that they can charm their circle of friends and family.

Their restless nature makes it easier for them to enjoy new experiences they can explore with their senses and adventurous activities. A typical Sag is a great traveler who has stories and tales of trips to new places that spices up their conversation. They are sincere people who may come off as blunt because they don't see the need to be diplomatic. The statement "Say it as it is" is typical with a Sagittarius.

Sagittarius individuals place a high value on friendships and the relationships they nurture in their lives. Ever willing to lend a listening and compassionate ear to people who need advice and described as lovely people who are kindhearted.

Although they are friendly and helpful, they can also be steadfast concerning how people deal with them. They will not demand compliance but will not fail to deal with people who are disrespectful towards them.

Those born under this sign have an open mind which makes them the right fit for the term "Global Citizen," they can switch from one state of mind to another without flinching. Most striking is the fact that they would do anything for a loved one.

Capricorn (December 22-January 19)
Passion is the keyword we use to describe a typical Capricorn; they want to achieve so much in life because they are born with dreams. They can be a bit shy, especially when they are amid new persons, but the moment they strike a connection with you, their fun side shines through.

Capricorns love to prove people wrong hence the reason for their ambitious nature. If something is unachievable before they got on the scene, they will strive to get it done and not run away from the challenge.

A Capricorn will dedicate himself/herself to work tirelessly. They will experience burnout from exhaustion and go right back to the same work the following day like they nothing happened the previous day.

One fun aspect of the Capricorn is that they value the people they love and are FIERCELY protective of them. They would do anything to make those they like to feel safe.

They have so much love to give, and they have a very pure heart (especially when you don't get in the way of their success). Unlike other signs who find it difficult staying alone, a typical Capricorn enjoys his/her company.

They crave close-knit friendships and make an effort to go out with friends, but once they are out, they desire to silence and want to go home. Capricorns are caring but do not hesitate to cut you off if you get on their wrong side.

Capricorns are loyal, they stand for what they believe in, and they are the perfect mix of sturdy but soft on the inside. They are funny yet sarcastic. One thing is sure, if you want good advice, call a Capricorn, you will get a direct answer with no hidden messages.

Which horoscope are you compatible with?

We all desire successful relationships; it feels good when knowing you've struck a connection with someone else who is just "Right" for you, but this can only be possible when you both are compatible. But they are brave enough to face daunting challenges and win.

Being compatible means two or more people can exist and work together with little or no conflict. Even when there are differences, the parties involved feeling free to voice their opinion and work out their problems.

There are different ways for people to be compatible, but for those who are concerned about the astrological aspect, zodiac signs mean a lot. It is often advised that you date someone compatible with your sign as a lot of relationship disasters can be avoided when this happens.

More excitedly is the fact that there is not just one sign of being compatible with yours, you will discover that for your sign there are probably two or three more signs, you have a fuller pool of individuals to seek out to get your perfect match.

So what are the compatible astrological signs?

Aquarius
Gemini and Libra are your compatibility signs! These three signs enjoy being around people yet they do not take their freedom/independence lightly. They always crave alone times with themselves as such this wouldn't be a problem for a Gemini or Libra who dates an Aquarius, they understand the need to be alone most times.

Aquarius, Libra, and Gemini don't conform to the societal norms and rules for dating as they allow each other explore freely, travel alone and are even thrilled with the idea of having separate bedrooms within the house. If an Aquarius is lucky to find a Gemini or a Libra, then they are fortunate to find someone who understands them inside and out.

Pisces
For Pisces, you are compatible with Scorpio and Cancer. You will feel drawn to individuals who are within the Scorpio and Cancer signs as this is the best way of ensuring a long-lasting relationship. Due to the shared water signs, you will have an understanding of each other's moods.

Now, this doesn't that the three signs are moody; it just means that they are certainly not the easiest of the signs out there. Most people think "High maintenance" when they remember the connection between these signs, but if the

Pisces finds Scorpio or Cancer, his/her emotions can be easily expressed.

The relationship between these signs will most likely succeed long-term because each sign has the freedom to be expressive with the other, which is a major feature of successful relationships.

Aries

An Aries is compatible with Leo, Gemini, Aquarius and Sagittarius. Aries have a magnetic persona, and although they can be very competitive with a bit of a control streak, they are very lovable. When an Aries shows up at a party, that is when the party starts, and if they host a party, everyone will want to get an invite.

A lot of signs are compatible with Aries except for Aries itself because you will be putting two people together who have too much energy. So Leo, Gemini, Aquarius, and Sagittarius are the perfect match.

Taurus

Taurus is most suited for Virgo and Pisces. Taurus are mostly known for their stubbornness, but in truth, they are very determined people who are motivated to achieve more. They like to get things done and tend to succeed because they are proactive with life.

This strength displayed by Taurus is what makes them a perfect match for Virgo and Pisces because the signs are also powerful. Virgo is hardworking and determined; Pisces has the strength of character.

So romance between a Taurus and Virgo or Pisces is one that will be delightful and very exciting for the parties involved.

Gemini

Aquarius and Libra are compatible signs with Gemini. The two-personality side of Gemini can be very challenging.

Geminis are sweet, so they appeal to Libra and Aquarius since these are signs that live on attention and affection.

The most suitable way of these two signs on your right side is to lavish them with love like they are the only ones in the world. Gemini also does well with other Geminis because they can handle each other and understand each other correctly.

Cancer
A Cancer is suitable with Scorpio and Pisces. Cancers can be very jealous because they absorb themselves in a lot of romantic movies and stories, Scorpio and Pisces help bring them down to reality.
Scorpio pays attention to details and can diffuse jealousy while Pisces although also romantic like the Cancer brings an even tone to the relationship, thus making it a smooth affair.

Cancer loves drama, and Pisces can be dramatic when the moment demands it so instead of treating Cancer like one who is attention seeking, Pisces enables the sign to be the best version of themselves.

Leo
Leos work best in relationships with Libra, Gemini, Aries, and Sagittarius. Leos are quite demanding when it comes to relationships and issues of love so that these signs can put up with their behavior. Lions like to think that they can run the entire connection so they like to be treated like royalty.

Sagittarius, Libra, and Gemini have no problems treating the Leo like royalty, Aries might have some difficulty with that expectation. However, Leo and Aries work because they pose a challenge to each other (the lion and ram staring down at each other) thus inspiring a desire for more love and life.

Virgo
A Virgo is most suited for a Taurus and Capricorn. Virgo is an Earth sign, so it is crucial that they also stick to other earth signs such as Capricorn and Taurus. These signs complement each other, but they also share a practical approach to what life has to offer them.

Practical people always go well together, when a Virgo and Taurus or Capricorn meet for their first date, their actual conversations may seem boring to other signs, but it can also be a moment the stars align for them to embark on a sweet, satisfying relationship.

Libra
A Libra is compatible with Leo and Sagittarius. There is a peaceful harmony with the Libra that makes it a beautiful sign for other signs. A Libra can come into your chaotic life and sweep you off your feet, bringing harmony and excitement.

For Leo, he/she will enjoy a relationship with a Libra because they both have a love for the beautiful things of life. Libra can also build a successful relationship with another Libra, thus creating a very peaceful and beautiful relationship.

Scorpio
Scorpio is most compatible with another Scorpio or Pisces. This combination may seem like an unusual choice, but there is a high level of success with their relationships. Their relationships with these signs are often filled with love and happiness, making it one of the most potent unions between the signs.

Two Scorpios coming together will enjoy each other's secretive nature, problem-solving skills, and a love for discovering the truth while fighting for justice. Pisces also works well with a Scorpio because they both have a peculiar nature; only both of them can appreciate about each other.

Both Pisces and Scorpio are fearless in their devotion to love as such being in a relationship together will be an exciting experience with the two of them devoted to each other for as long as the relationship lasts.

Sagittarius
A Sagittarius is compatible with Libra, Aquarius, Leo, and Aries. Now, Sagittarius do get bored quickly yet they can keep things sweet and spicy, which is a trait the other signs find endearing. Although Leos like to talk and think about themselves, they tend to make the situation boring, which is why a Sagittarius has to come in to strike a balance.

Capricorn
Capricorns and Taurus are both earthy signs, which makes them a perfect match. They are both passionate signs with an appreciation of each other's approach towards life.

Taurus place high importance on money and the same with Capricorn, Taurus also appreciates the dedication and hard work of Capricorn, making the relationship a loving and supportive one.

Capricorn admires ambitions. Since Taurus is also an achiever, both signs will build a bad marriage where there is mutual respect for the effort they both put into the union.

Taurus and Capricorn also believe in doing things the right way even if they have to stand alone, so this is another reason why they are a perfect match. They will argue in the relationship but will quickly get over it because they have an intense connection

Another sign that is compatible with Capricorn is Pisces. With both signs, it is a case of "Opposite attracts," and their differences will serve as a beneficial factor to the relationship.

While Capricorn helps Pisces to establish a sense of security, Pisces helps Capricorn lighten up enough to have some fun. A union between Capricorn and Pisces has excellent potential with the individual's strengths and weaknesses at the fore of the relationship.

Virgo is also compatible with Capricorn; they both love to succeed and will be great role models for other couples. Their practical nature of finance will help them make the right money decisions.

Virgos and Capricorns are also hardworking people who will always inspire each other to do better with their work and careers. Both signs also have the same kind of social life where they don't spend time with so many people.

Both Virgo and Capricorn will enjoy a lot of date nights and spend time together instead of going out with other friends or couples.

There is a need for you to understand why the signs placed the way they are concerning relationships, so we are taking this journey a step further with the content in the next chapter.

Chapter Three
Understanding Relationships

Chapter two was a buildup from chapter one and a way of sharing the most fundamental approaches about astrology. You will need an understanding of how it works and how it applies to your life hence the reason for this chapter.

Now we are shifting the compass to the concept of gaining an understanding of how astrology affects your relationships. We all care about the people we connect it, and it is innate in us to ponder away thinking about the people that become the object of our affections.

Questions always reign supreme in our minds such as, is this person right for me? Should I be dating this person? Would we make a formidable pair? What if we break up?

These questions will never go away until you settle for the right person. So the best thing you can do is getting answers, and astrology has the best solutions for you.

Astrology is like a mirror when you look at it, it shows you what is real, so where else will you get the answers you need concerning a relationship partner?

So in this chapter, you are going to get a comprehensive look at the relationship aspect of astrology. This aspect will enable you to get answers to the questions you seek.

In this section, you will also find ideas on how you can make the right decisions about the people you love.

For you to fully grasp the idea of relationships and astrology, you must know what it means to have a twin soul. A twin soul is that one person in the world that you connect with a deeper level and you believe is your soulmate.

The relationship you have with this individual is never perfect, but both of you continually strive to get better at it. The most beautiful thing about this relationship is that you wouldn't give up on each other.

Some people never meet their twin souls, so they settle for someone they have feelings for and someone right for the moment. For some other persons, they don't care how long they have to wait; their search continues till they find the "One."

But with astrology, you wouldn't have to wait for a very long time. When you know the signs that are just right for you and the ones you are most compatible with, it saves you the stress of a general search.

Astrology empowers you with the right set of information that will allow you to search for your twin soul and get positive results. So when an attraction takes place between two compatible signs, what happens is that their sun signs and ascendants meet.

Which means that Sun and Ascendant cause attraction between two persons while the Moon, Venus, and Mars are the determining factor for the strength of the connection, which ultimately sustains the relationship.
Some important aspects of synastry

Interaction between the Sun, Moon, and Venus creates a powerful attraction between two people; the elements between Venus and Mars indicate sexual attraction. The intense aspects between Venus and Mars create a strong sexual attraction that mostly presents challenges to the relationship.

The Trine and Sextile aspects between both planets create a blend of energies, but sometimes the relationship might become too comfy for the parties involved making it very dull.

The aspects between the Moon and Venus or Mars show if the two people are emotionally in tune with each other. The tense aspects can cause a strain on the relationship, thus preventing the parties from relating to each other on an intimate level.

Houses

We cannot complete our astrological analysis of relationships without talking about the interplay of houses between two charts that determines the role of the individuals cast on each other concerning the planets.

When we compare birth charts, the planets in the 1st, 5th, 7th, and 8th houses are significant because these are the houses that have love themes. When some of your planets fall in the 1st, 5th, 7th and 8th houses of your potential partner's card, an intimate relationship is undoubtedly in the cards. So what do the houses represent in synastry?

The 1st House (Ascendant)
Our outer personality is ruled by the 1st house; attraction happens when we discover someone whose image and character is appealing to us. When planets enter the first house of another person's chart, there will be a strong attraction between both parties.

The 5th House
The 5th house rules over pleasure and romance; if there are a lot of planets in the 5th house or that of the partners in a relationship, there is bound to be a strong bond of friendship. The two persons involved will enjoy similar activities and possess the same likes and dislikes.

The 7th House (Descendant)
This house rules relationships and partnerships; it is an essential house for marriages, if one person's planets occupy the 7th house of his/her partner, it will most likely lead to a successful marriage.

The 8th House
This house rules sex, and depending on the planet occupying it at a time, the person might feel the urge to control his/her partner. Obsessive tendencies are also portrayed by the person whose planet holds their partner's 8th house. When planets occupy the 8th house, you can be sure of an intense attraction towards each other.

Through the concept of synastry, the dynamics of relationships and love is understood. A lot of things affect the course of our lives, but the contact we make with others has a more profound effect as such synastry should be considered with an open mind.

The knowledge of synastry you've read entails the fundamental principles of what defines love and relationships from an astrological standpoint for you get an accurate assessment of any partnership you must consider all aspects of synastry.

Before we get on to the next idea which is a detailed explanation on your best days for romance and friendship, you should know that there is also a connection between the proximity of your sign and that of your partner, lets quickly consider that shall we?

Relationship between those who share the same sign is always easy-going because both parties feel like they are looking in the mirror and seeing their strengths and weakness.

The relationships between those who are one sign apart are likened to a teacher-student relationship. One party has to allow the other to take the lead, an example of such ties entails a Cancer and a Leo or Aries and a Taurus.

For people who are twos signs apart, friendship is the bedrock of the relationship, even when faced with severe challenges that could result in A breakup, friendship keeps them together. Examples are a Virgo and Scorpio or a Gemini and Leo.

For those who are dating with three signs apart, it can be a very tensed relationship, but it can be managed, examples are a Pisces and Capricorn or a Sagittarius and Aquarius.

If you are dating four signs apart, then the relationship will flow naturally and effortlessly, you both will feel like you are made for each other. Examples of this combination include Gemini and Libra or Taurus and Capricorn.

For relationships that are five signs apart, there will be some challenges with communication, but if there is love at the heart of the partnership, you both will be fine. Examples include Virgo and Aries or Libra and Pisces.

Your Best Days for Romance & Friendships

Picture this!

You are in the same fancy restaurant you've always desired to go to with a date, there is a lit candle on the table, and you are with this young man who is everything you've dreamed about in a partner. At that instant you are wondering, "My stars must have aligned, is this really happening?"

It seems like nothing could go wrong at that moment until three days after the date you discover that your date has blocked you on all social media platforms, and you never get another text after sending several.

This is the story of a typical dating experience for a young man or woman, sometimes it feels like it's all "Trial and Error" until you find the ONE that makes it work.

It would be helpful if you gained some insight into the best times for you to get into the dating pool and meet someone who responds to text after three days. Of course, you might want to get to know if the person is compatible with you (get to know their birthdays and do the astrological math using the details in Chapter Two).

But aside from knowing if they are a match, you need to know if the timing is right for you as well. Now the planets are never static (don't we all wish they were?), which means that your chances tends to change as they move and the energy around them.

So it would be quite daunting to tell you to dress up on a Monday or Tuesday because that's the exact day for love and friendship. What we can do is give you your predictions for love this year based on the movement of the planets and your peculiar astrological sign.

This is the one section of this book that is subject to change because if you read this material in 2020, the report for you might be different. You could seek out an astrologer later to give you details based on what's happening with the planet at that time.

So what is the best time for love for you in 2019? Are you going to make new friends? Yes, a considerable part of the year is gone already but don't worry now, you will get an accurate reading that matches the remaining portion of the year.

Aries
This year you will be focused on yourself and your career so you might not get any new or lasting romantic life partners, but that is fine. Regardless, you are going to have fun with the people you meet.

But if you are still focused on love and want to meet someone have an open mind about it, go after new options now and look forward to August, it is a particular month for some spice and sugar in your life.

Taurus
If you are looking for someone special this year then you are in luck, you will find someone new or someone from the past for a long term relationship. It will be exciting, powerful, and quite sudden too. It may have felt like you will never find this one true soulmate, but this is a good time for that to happen.

Jupiter will spill the golden dust on your partnerships as the sky lights up your House of intimacy, take the time to consider what you give in the relationship and what you receive while communicating your desires to the other person. Open your heart this year; it is ready for love!

Gemini
Oh, Geminis should get ready for this is the year of love for them! The previous years you spent attaining spiritual growth will lead you to situations where you connect with a potential partner.

Put the years of struggling for love behind you for good because the universe is about to open some doors for you. Jupiter is the blessed planet for luck and fortune, and it will be moving through your House of Marriage and Commitment all through this year until December 3.

You will find someone who likes to go an adventure with you, and this person will be willing to commit by taking the relationship to the next level. If you are already in a beautiful relationship or marriage, then things are certainly looking up for the two of you.

Cancer
2019 is the year for you to find true love if you have worked on yourself in the past year, so you are about to form new spiritual friendships, great career relationships with favorable business ties. Beyond the romance spectrum, your relationships will all have a positive boost this year.

There will be three significant eclipses in your House of Marriage and partnership this year, which means if you are single, finding the right person will feature more prominently in your mind than ever before.

Three dates look great for you this year 2019, January 5 (a day for open doors for love to happen) which leads to July 16 and then on December 26, these dates will pave the way for happier relationships so do look out for December, it will be memorable!

Leo
Your potential for love is high this year, but this will only happen when you make specific changes in your life that will enable you to become a bit more flexible. Jupiter is the planet of miracles, and it is dancing through your House of Love and Romance until December 3.

You are the luckiest of the signs to find love so go out there and radiate your irresistible light so that special one can be drawn to you.

Virgo
In 2019, you will meet and connect with long-term romantic prospects, but you must be discerning and have clarity with your intentions so the relationship (if it happens) can flow in harmony.

Lead with your heart this year if you are keen on finding someone special. This year you will have three eclipses in your House of True Love and with your Romance which takes place on January 5 (past), July 16 (already past) and December 26.

Be conscious of the New Moon on August 30 as well as you watch the kind of love life you want to be manifested. Don't worry if you missed out on any date already, there is something special for you this year, and it would happen!

Libra

If your birthday falls at the latter part of the Libra sign (around October 20-22), then you have a higher chance of meeting someone special this year. But first work on the issues you had with past relationships and your sense of identity.

2019 will be right for you because you will be at the center of your world, give your partner extra affection because Mars will be empowering you from February 14.

Scorpio

You had great luck with love 2017 because Jupiter is your sign, but this year it is about creating more wealth. Don't worry about love, it is in the stars for you already, focus on the influence of the moon to help you get new contacts for stronger friendships.

Someone who has marriage on the cards for you will come your way this year, but you must keep your faith up for a love that will be all yours.

Sagittarius

In 2019 you will most likely meet someone you connect with on a higher and spiritual level, but for this to become a relationship, you need to be clear on your intentions.

Stop repeating this statement "I don't know, let's see if it works out" when you meet someone you have a secure connection with.

Jupiter will be giving you more luck this year, so it is a good time for partnerships from now till December. If you have the desire to spice up your marriage or relationship, this is a great year to make that happen.

Also set the intention for what you want with your love life so the universe can provide that, it is the beginning of an excellent chapter in your life, embrace it!

Capricorn
This is the year for you to concentrate on the long-term vision. There are three significant eclipses in your sign and a significant indication for marriage or stronger partnerships from July (precisely the 2nd day in July).

This year is a big one for you as your destiny is about to take a better turn with love. If you don't have anyone stable in your life right now, create a list of what you want in a partner and be on the lookout. But don't worry, 2019 is a good year for you, and you will surely have a blast.

Aquarius
2019 seems like a causal year for you, you will meet lots of new people, but the chances of striking a great connection doesn't seem very high at this time. Jupiter will be moving through House of Friendships, so it will be great for you to go out with friends more often.

Meet new people without having your hopes high, ask your friends to introduce you to new people as this is bound to bring more luck into your life. So it seems temporarily bleak with love BUT, it is an excellent year for friendship for you, enjoy that!

Pisces
There is good news for love for those under these signs; you will most likely meet someone that you've got a great connection with this year. Since you are known for your whimsical nature, do not leap into a relationship speedily.

Take your time this year to get to know the person before committing to him/her. To get the best out of your search this year, focus on the middle of August through to September as it is an excellent time to get a great partner.

The celestial bodies will also bring you luck in the wedding department, write down what you want in a partner and take those steps because it's all looking good for you this year.

Please note that the predictions above are based on your general readings from your signs. You can get a personalized reading when you visit an astrologer who uses the details shared in the beginning part of this chapter on Synastry to get a more precise date.

More so, some signs have a better chance of meeting "The one" faster than others, but this doesn't mean you wouldn't find love this year. Keep an open mind, stay focused, and whether you meet that special one in 2019 or not, you will surely find happiness in your world.

How to Bring Positive Energy To Your Relationships

We spend a large chunk of our time seeking love and wondering when we will find "The one," now that you know what to look out for this year you must also understand that relationships are just what they are, SHIPS!

You are going to get on board with this other person who has a different background and lifestyle with you, meaning there is bound to be challenges and issues as you move at sea. There will be calm winds and then rough ones too.
Watch your relationship circle
Sometimes, neither you nor your partner contributes to the negative energy you experience in your relationship. The

evil power is attributed to the kind of people you let into your lives.

There is the concept of "Date night" in the world today where couples go out together to spend quality time, could be a gaming night or dinner at a restaurant.
The point is that if you're always hanging out with couples who have a negative approach to life, you will begin to manifest their negativity too.

So the first step to take towards restoring positive energy in your relationship is for you to assess the people you and your partner spend time together. If you realize that you don't have shared positive values, then there is no need for such friendships.

Be a support system
Negative triumphs in your relationship when you don't become your partner's support system. In most relationships, this is the singular problem; they are having that keeps rearing its ugly head and the source of consistent arguments.

But consider the bright side, if you do become each other's support, there is every guarantee that the fights will stop. There will be better harmony between you and your partner.

Harmony is a product of positive energy; it is an excellent foundation on which you can build a long-lasting union that will be an inspiration to all others. So as you read through this section, start thinking about ways through which you can show more support for your partner.

Could you be more caring about his/her work challenges? Can you use reassuring words to let your partner know that you will always be there for him/her?

A partner who is a support system brings a lot of positive energy to the relationship. Yes, there will still be interpersonal challenges, but you will realize that your life is with your relationship is better. You and your partner will have a delightful union with you two supporting each other.

Be a good listener
Sometimes when we say there is negative energy in our relationships what we are saying is that one party isn't doing enough. Both parties need to put in the work to make each other feel special.

Sometimes when your partner comes to you with a problem he/she doesn't want advice, they may wish to a listening ear and be free to pour their heart out.

By being available for your partner, you can take away the negativity in your relationship and replace it with positive energy. More importantly, when you listen to your partner, do not listen to give a reply, you should listen to understand first.

Even if your partner isn't a good listener, you can teach him/her to become one by being a good listener yourself. Start by always asking your partner at the end of each day how his/her day went. As simple as this question is, it will mean a lot and show that you care.

As you listen to your partner, the easier it becomes for you two to grow closer in love. Keep the negative vibes at bay and genuinely enjoy the bliss of a happy relationship.

Now even if your astrological sign reads that you are not patient with listening, make an effort with your partner. The effort might make a big difference in your relationship.

So when the other person doesn't seem to conform to the changes we want for ourselves (which is selfish by the way) we throw fists, tantrums, use hurtful words and even try to blackmail the person emotionally.

You can enjoy a peaceful relationship irrespective of your astrological ties by being conscious of the fact that we are all different and our differences make the world an exciting place.

You are trying to change this person because you only concentrate on his/her flaws, which is an unfair analysis. Try to list the person' strengths, and you will be amazed at a depth of their personality.

Accept them for who they are to you, accept their little awkward gestures and love them for the value, joy, and peace they bring to your life. You would be doing this for the sake of your relationship and for your inner peace.

Use positive words
Negative words yield negative results in any relationship, and you know what these words are, any word that causes strife, pain, anger, or bitterness will be replaced with kind and helpful words.
Use affirmations to say the right things about your partner, if you think that your partner lacks a particular trait that will also help him/her get better in life, speak it forth into the universe.

When you make it a habit to use positive words, you will start to feel the negative energy slowly ebb away. From your relationship and positive energy swiftly returning, it will be such a fantastic experience.

Avoid the pitfalls of comparison
Comparisons are a deal-breaker for any relationship, and they are the easiest ways of ensuring that negativity thrives with your partner. Listen to this; there will always be somebody better there who looks better, smiles excellently, and even has more money.

But you chose your partner; you made your choice backed by the universe, so don't compare him/her with someone else. Keep the positive energy within your relationship on lock like an airtight bag. Continue to reaffirm all the good in your partner, and that is what you will get in return.

Express gratitude
Sometimes you need to put things in perspective and be grateful for what you have; this will help you realize that you do have a lot of things to be thankful for instead of things you fight over.

Every relationship is dynamic, and while it is healthy to have expectations, don't forget to be appreciative of your journey thus far and your partner. There is a time for constructive criticism, and there is a time for gratitude.

Gratitude, when released is a positive energy that can breathe some freshness into your relationship. Regardless of your partner's zodiac sign, he/she would love to hear words of gratitude for good things done in the partnership.

So quit complaining (negative energy), nagging (negative energy) or any other activity that causes you to have a frown on your face. Smile always even through the storm it is what life within the astrological circle is about (positive energy).

A general solution for more positive energy in your relationship will be for you to study your partner's sign to learn more about his/her personality and then try to do things that excite the individuals.

Leos love an adventure, Capricorns love a good challenge, these are some examples, learn more about your partner from an astrological perspective, and you will get great ideas on how you can infuse positive energy into your relationship.

Why Are You Struggling With Relationships?

For some people, their relationship struggles are not about concepts such as "Energy," they have issues with knowing who they are and building relationships that match their unique personalities.

We are going to round off this section by providing insight into the reasons why you may be struggling with your relationships from an astrological viewpoint. When you know these peculiar details about yourself, you will be better prepared for any relationship and nothing will take you by surprise.

Aquarius
Your head is always in the clouds, dreaming and you struggle in relationships when you sense that your partner is trying to control or manipulate you.

Due to your independent attitude, you tend to be emotionally detached sometimes, and this can be a struggle if you are with a partner that isn't mentally capable of managing your independence and taking it in good strides.

Pisces
These are the most emotional people, and it is both good and bad for their relationships. You express all feelings with intensity, and this also shows your inability to handle emotional crises, which can be overwhelming for your partner.

Aries
You are a good listener and love to show excessive affection, which can make your partner feel suffocated. Your partner tends to withdraw when he/she feels

smothered by you, and that's when the relationship hits the rocks.

Taurus
Taurus is a loyal sign and very devoted to his/her partner, but the problem is that they struggle with forgiveness after they are betrayed. They hold on to wrongdoings of their partners, and over time, the partner gets tired of apologizing and trying to prove that there is change.

Gemini
Geminis are flirts and struggle with consistency in relationships. They love adventure, so when they are with one partner and feel like it is starting to get boring, they quickly jump ship and look for more "Exciting" game.

So for a typical Gemini finding love is easy; staying in love and accepting the inevitable boring routines that come with one partner is the challenge.

Cancer
Stop hiding behind a tough shell while you are sweet and sensitive on the inside; you are struggling because you don't want to open up and trust someone. Quite disturbing, is the fact that you hold on to previous relationships for years, and this doesn't help you see new prospects the universe has sent your way.

Leo
Leos have a big ego, they don't compromise easily, and relationships are all about compromises. Leos only struggle at the start of a relationship, but if you start trusting your partner, you will open up easily and build a long-term relationship.

Virgo
Virgos are perfectionists, and relationship prospects often feel uncomfortable around them because of the pressure to be perfect. Of course, it helps you figure out the ones

that are serious and will take a chance, but on the other hand, no one likes to be analyzed and criticized at every turn.

Libra
You have a loving nature, but your struggle is with the fact that you are too giving hence the reason you don't have any boundaries. You must create borders, or you will continue to lose relationships and move from one to another.

Scorpio
This is one of the most intense signs hence the reason they are tagged as having am fiery mood, which also makes them unforgiving individuals. When their partners offend them, it takes a lot for a Sagittarius to accept the partner back, and this can be a real struggle in relationships.

Sagittarius
Sagittarius are lustful people, and this causes them to make mistakes by thinking they love someone when they are just sensual for the person. You fall in love with someone and give them you're all so when they are with the wrong person; it is easy to take advantage of their feelings.

Capricorn
The reason you struggle in your relationships is that you are consumed with the idea of getting married and starting a family that you don't spend time thinking if the person you are with is the right person for you.

You are also driven by "Status" and always want to maintain a particular appearance regardless of what the reality is so you strive to make your relationship look perfect on the outside even when it is in turmoil on the inside.

Astrology is all around us, it is in the air we breathe, and in our relationships, for you to get the best out of every relationship, you must be conscious of the astrological interpretations of your signs and that of your partner (even potential partners).

We are still on our journey towards unraveling more on the connection between astrology and your life, what are we taking on with the next chapter? Finances!

When all is well with you from work, career to the relationship, you will also want to ensure that the same "Wellness" applies to your financial capacity. Learn more about this idea in the next chapter.

Astrological predictions varies based on the movement of the planets, things can change in an instant. The content of this chapter is to enlighten you on the possibilities you have to make the right friendships and create the right relationships based on what the universe wants for you.

Chapter Four
Astrology & Your Finances

Money!

Financial independence!

Access to wealth!

The statements above will get anyone's attention regardless of age, gender, or race because money is a universal concept. Why do you wake up early in the morning, rush off the kids to school and head to the office? It's because you are in search of money.

Why will anyone have multiple streams of income and continue to seek out more? It's all because money is a driver of ideas and the tool we use to manifest our dreams.

But there are several layers to the monetary concept; there is the aspect of acquisition which constitutes the concept of earning, there is also the aspect of availability which entails having the monies you need to execute projects.

Then there is the aspect of continuance, which involves seeking ways to have continued access to funds through outlets such as investments, savings etc.

Now all of these concepts and ideas about money are relatable to all of us because it is something we deal with daily. You should also know that the manner in which you execute these ideas and the rationale behind your monetary decision making process is linked to your astrological sign.

By now, you already know that everything is linked to your sign as we have successfully shown you the link between astrology and your personality, relationships, and now finances. In the next chapter, you will discover the connection between astrology and your positive/negative traits.

So the point is, just as astrology has a deep-rooted connection with these aspects of your life, so it is with your finances. Some signs have a flexible approach towards money, while others can be efficient. First you need to figure out what your sign says and then work towards enhancing the positive and working on making the negative better.

We don't have to spend so much time on the preamble, let' get right to it!

What you should know about money and your sign

Aries

You are known for your impulsiveness and carelessness with money, although you are competitive which makes you earn well, you don't make the right financial decisions all the time.

You enjoy the thrill of a fast-paced career that keeps you on your toes and comes with a lot of financial benefits. Your impulsive nature makes it quite difficult for you to save or work with a budget.

However, you quickly bounce back from financial challenges hence the reason you are also able to switch jobs rapidly in the early days of your career.

You like to take risks with investments but be mindful of the kind of investments that may seem excellent and right on the surface but terrible with profitability long-term.

You tend to know when your bank account is negatively affected by your negative purchases and know when to take a break from buying items.

Capricorn

You are ambitious, a hard worker, and very competitive; hence, the reason you have a high probability of making money quickly. Your wealth creation will take a while because you love to work your way up in your career, so the later part of your life holds a lot of financial promise.

You are always striving for financial attainment, and you are practical with money; hence, the reason you save a lot. The people close to you may be worried that you are too frugal with your finances because of a decreased tendency to make unnecessary purchases.

Unlike other signs, you don't place importance on buying new clothes or going to excellent restaurants. You would rather spend money on things that reflect how successful you are and how far you've come.

You can be quite conservative with your investment choices, going for investment ideas that will pay in the future as you are not in a hurry to get results now. A typical Capricorn should learn to step outside of his/her comfort zone occasionally and take risks (it adds some spice to life).

Your significant goal financially is to be secure; hence, the reason you are careful with money. You can be thoughtful with your purchases, so the idea of buying things spontaneously is alien to you.

Instead of buying an expensive item, you would rather save the money for future purposes. Your practical nature makes it easier for you to do well with finances even better than other signs.

You are very good at achieving results, so your place at the top of the corporate ladder is secure. Although quite commendable, your frugal nature can become a problem because you would tend to deprive yourself of specific things to save and plan for the future.

Think about today, you are here, while planning for the future always have today in mind and do what makes you happy even if you have to spend money.

Taurus

Taurus has a dependable nature; thus, they are very good with money. Individuals born under this sign are very stable hence the reason they like to plan for the future.

They make financial plans and stick to it long-term making them one of the most steadfast individuals concerning financial responsibility. You like beautiful things and want to indulge yourself, which is the reason you work very hard and love to make money.

You are great at spending money even though you have problems budgeting. You don't want anyone to tell you that you can't have what you need. You are extravagant, generous and very considerate with the gifts

One of the most exciting things about a Taurus is the fact that he/she can manage money well enough so when personal spending is going overboard, they can put a stop to it.

You are practical with money; hence, the reason you are conscious of financial risks and put measures in place to protect your economic interests.

You feel better knowing that there is a back-up account or savings somewhere that will help you on rainy days. With investments, you love long-term investments that pay off eventually, and you are also outstanding at real estate investments.

Gemini

Geminis are quite engaging, and their double-sided nature has an impact on their finances. You are motivated by money and luxury; hence, the reason you make a lot of impulsive purchases.

There is a side of you that is impulsive, likes to gamble and the other side that is financially sound, you can't tell which side will dominate, so it depends on the level of control you have over your personality.

Be mindful of the kind of financial goals you set for yourself so you can be sure of sticking to them. You can also set up deposits for your retirement account while allowing yourself to have fun.

Saving money can be a challenge for you, and this is because you are optimistic about bouncing back when faced with financial difficulty. Due to the varied interests you have, you are prone to switch jobs more often than expected, and this can affect your finances.

You are smart and dynamic, which makes it easier for you to discover lucrative ways of making money. Overall you may still need the help of an accountant who will manage your finances and cause you to make the best decisions.

Pisces

You are practical with money, which means that savings are natural with you, and you also love a tremendous high-income career path. You have a good heart, which makes you help people even when it isn't convenient for you to do so.

You must be mindful of this trait though; most Pisces find that they end up paying more than they can afford for someone else to help out, and this isn't a wise money decision.

You also have a loose relationship with money; hence, the reason you are focused on debts, taxes, or other crucial financial issues that may cause troubles for you later.

Instead of being ignorant of these issues, reach out to a financial expert who can help you take care of them, so you are not held down by tax challenges.

You have to also work on your compassionate nature by making sure no one takes advantage of that, be kind but smart about it. You like to spend money going to the movies, music concerts, museums, and art collections.

You are not thrifty, and you don't like being on a budget either, but if staying on a budget will help you in challenging times, you are open to the idea.

Take an active interest in what happens to your finances and avoid making emotional, financial decisions because it is in your nature to be sensitive. If you are faced with a business challenge, you cannot handle, reach out to an expert for help.

Leo

Due to your charisma and leadership skills, you will make a great entrepreneur, and this also means that earning money wouldn't be a challenge for you. But you love the most delicate things of life and have great taste for luxury.

Your desire for big brands and the luxurious life can cause friction between what you earn and this lifestyle you want to uphold. You are also protective of friends and families hence the reason for your immense generosity.

However, you need to ensure that your generosity doesn't cause a conflict between your financial security and your desire to make life easier for others (create some economic boundaries)

You don't have a problem with savings occasionally (not consistently), which is excellent because your great taste in material things can only be checked through savings. You enjoy making money and working hard while advancing your business or career.

You are always faced with situations where you buy things you cannot afford so download money-saving apps or use discount codes when shopping to keep that tendency in check.

You are a bit impulsive when it comes to gifting other items because you like to show people how special they are, which makes you can go all out for them (designer clothes, jewelry, etc.).

Your first choice of an investment may be with jewelry and the more beautiful things in life you want to indulge in because these are the things that make you feel good about yourself.

Virgo

You are hardworking and quite practical with your finances, which is the reason for your savings set aside for retirement, a car, or a house. You are always selective about what you buy and try to limit your purchasing impulsiveness.

While these characteristics mentioned above are excellent, it prevents you from enjoying the proceeds of your hard work. You get to have good financial health but feel restricted because you are worried about the future.

You are also very selfless hence the reason you can remain in a low-paying job because you think it will help you make a difference in the lives of other people.

For your investment angle, you are unwilling to jump at every opportunity that seems to hold the promise of profit or massive turnover. Instead, you will take on extensive research to be sure of your decision before taking the plunge.

Your frugal nature also prompts you to have a budget for everything, and you wouldn't spend money until it was necessary for you to do so. You always keep an eye on where your money goes through financial journals and other measures that keep you grounded financially.

Here is some advice, go out more often and relax, you can save for the future and remain financially responsible while making out time for fun. Buy the dress you love, and enjoy some little guilty pleasures occasionally.

Also, don't be afraid to take risks (calculated risks), you will make great financial choices because you are keen on research, so don't be scared to do something unconventional. You will not fail at it; you will only learn vital life and financial lessons in the process

Scorpio

Scorpios are focused and driven by everything about their lives, even money. They are incredibly meticulous with research, and they bring this trait into their finances as well, which makes them good at investing.

They can also be competitive, which makes them active at work as they pursue their career with determination; this doesn't go unnoticed at their workplaces.

Scorpios are all about control, making them quite decisive with financial decisions. They like to take risks and are not impulsive spenders, but their focus on finances can be too intense, consuming most of their time and energy.

Of course, you should work towards securing a future for yourself, but this doesn't mean you should be obsessed with money all the time. Take time off work and money concerns sometime to enjoy your life with the money you make so effortlessly.

You are good at finding get-rich-quick ideas that do not lead to long-term investment dividends, but you like to try your luck with these things. In most cases, the schemes work for you, so you stretch your chance and continue to apply this skill

Your instincts are your most substantial financial capability because you are always led in the right path with investment decisions. Due to your competitive nature, you also make money quickly, right after conquering one idea you are out for the next one.

The influence of your instincts also makes it easy for you to take on aggressive investment strategies after careful consideration. You tend to wait patiently for the "Right" time to make a move with investment, and you can be very secretive with the amount of money you have.

Scorpios are known for not divulging financial information about the money they have in the house, assets, and even money they have in their bank accounts. In some extreme cases, they wouldn't share the information with their spouses or partners.

You like to plan for the future because you don't want an unexpected event to take you by surprise. But even if you get into a financial predicament, your instincts will help you recover quickly as you will know the next move to take immediately.

Sagittarius

You love to travel! You are not always interested in material items because you prefer to have memorable experiences, and this is where you get to swipe your credit card more often.
As a Sagittarius, you place value on being free, and you love to express the same kind of freedom with your finances. Which means you try to avoid debt as much as possible (because it will hold you down).

You are always optimistic even in the face of challenges and impromptu changes, hence the reason you don't believe in saving funds. You think that when you find yourself in a tight corner, you can come out of it unscathed.

You have the determination and ability to achieve all of your financial goals, and while your optimism is admirable, you might want to take some proactive steps with your finances occasionally.

For example, try setting up your retirement and emergency accounts because you have to plan for the future. You can plan ahead and still set money aside monthly for your travels, fun activities, and the adventures you love.

Your relationship with money is often termed as "Easy" because you don't get worried like some of the other signs. You always feel like money will come around because of your optimistic nature, and in most cases, you are right.

Yes, you work hard, and you tend to let your steam and stress go with traveling, which keeps the "Money" pressure other people face off you. You are quick on your feet, thus making it easier for you to make a come-back after a financially stressful ordeal or problem.

As a Sagittarius, you are not solely focused on money; you only like to think about what you can do with cash and the things that money allows you to do.

You often switch jobs a lot, especially in your younger years hence the reason for working your way up a career may take a longer time, which affects your financial status at some point in your life.

The fact that you have a peculiar history of always getting money when you need it doesn't mean you should be unperturbed when there is a financial crisis, improve on your saving pattern.

Cancer

Cancer individuals have a love for family, home, and communal values; thus, they are fiercely protective of their family, which makes it convenient for them to be very good at saving money.

Because they are family-oriented individuals, they are aware that an emergency could spring forth at any time hence the reason they save consistently.

They also want to create an ideal and stable home for their family, prompting them always to seek ways to spend money on an aspect of the house that needs repairs swiftly.

Cancer sign people love to spend money on fun activities that will bring them closer to their families. So they initiate family trips, visiting friends, attending social events, etc.

They also strive to have a stable financial base so they can get their desired comfort. Which means they are not spontaneous spenders. They will instead carry out detailed research when they want to make a big purchase (furniture or a new gadget) than go to a shop to buy randomly.

In preparing for a big purchase, they will save towards it, try to get the best prices. Cancers take their mortgage and other housing financials seriously because they don't want anything happening to their home.

Cancers are willing to work twice as hard as anyone else even work at a job they don't like to ensure they have a stable financial income. You feel more relaxed knowing you've got something to fall back on (savings).

Your love for family and homes makes your investment choices tanked at real estate, your heart lies within a right home, so this becomes your obvious choice of investment.

You are keen on following your instincts when it comes to financial opportunities, and because you are always cautious with money, you tend to listen to your gut feeling about certain investments before committing.

You will only settle for an investment option that aligns with your passion and values, but this could make you miss out on other profitable investment opportunities that may come your way.

So while staying true to your passions, also try to have an open mind about investment, after all, it is all about taking calculated risks. By giving these other opportunities a chance, you will be giving yourself a chance at learning something new which "Could" be the next big thing.

Libra

You love life, so you don't mind splurging on the most beautiful things of life that cut across artworks, clothing, food, and any other item that catches your fancy. You love to treat yourself to a great meal in a fun restaurant; hence, the reason a large chunk of your finances goes into fine dining weekly or monthly.

A good portion of your income is also spent on luxury items that make you feel good about yourself, such as clothes, cars, or decorative furnishing to boost the interiors of your home or office.

When it comes to investments, other signs may prefer making financial investments, but you love to invest in what interests you. So your investment of choice is usually in art and other creative areas.

You are an excellent team player, which makes it easier for you to collaborate with other people to make financial decisions. But in some cases, you will need the help of a financial advisor that can help you build a more diverse investment portfolio because it is often not advisable that you invest in single platforms like the arts alone.

As a Libra, you also have a keen sense of balance with your finances, which means even when you are not working with a budget, you will most likely not overspend.

Within you, there are thoughts about saving for the rainy day, so you make sure to have funds set aside for that eventuality. Before buying something, you like to consider all angles, thus helping you make informed decisions.

Although there are a few times, you go with the flow of what you desire and purchase without any consideration. If you discover that you are making too many impulsive financial decisions at a fast rate, take a break and speak with a financial expert.

Sometimes with you, it is not about "What" you wish to buy but "Why" you want to buy it. Always ask yourself the "Why" question if you feel conflicted about a purchase.

Aquarius

Those under this sign make high income because they are dedicated, hardworking individuals who enjoy the meaningful work they do. They also tend to donate part of their earnings to charities and good causes because it is hard for them to watch people live in poverty.

Sharing your wealth always comes naturally to you, but you must be mindful about charitable donations, plan for them and take them on when you are sure you will still be fine financially (if you go broke who will help those people in need?).

Concerning investments, you tend to take on unique investment strategies that may seem too risky to others, but you are financially intelligent to know the ones that will yield results and the ones that will not.

Aquarius is also a genuine entrepreneur who is ambitious and hardworking; he/she takes innovations seriously and want to make life easier for others through the business solutions they design.

Their love for value-based businesses will attract money to them because people always pay for value. For a typical Aquarian being creative at work to succeed is part of a daily routine because as much as they like to give a lot, they also love to boost their earnings.

Aquarius individuals tend to save as well to strike a balance with their charitable acts and their desire to invest money. Overall, you have good intentions with cash, and you can make the right decisions too, but always strive for that "Balance."

It is possible to have all areas of your life in order from relationships to finances, yes you need to utilize the force that is astrology to gain insight into what the universe has for you and make decisions based on what you unearth.

Have you ever wondered what makes human beings so unique? Well, it isn't the fact that we hail from different nationalities; it is the undeniable truth in our personality that has the capacity for negative and positive traits at the same time.

It is time to delve more into the link between astrology and these traits we embody, flip over, and enjoy the read.

*Financial decisions should not be made solely on astrological predictions. Take all forecasts into consideration, but if you feel the need to speak to a financial expert, go right ahead to gain professional insight into how you can manage your financial assets.

Chapter Five
Revealing Your Positive & Negative Personality Traits

Geminis are known for their dual personality in one person; we tend to focus so much on this peculiar sign as their natural combination makes them quite fascinating. We don't know one of the two sides we will be dealing with at a time, so it gives off an anticipatory feel backed by an element of surprise.

But why do we focus so much on Geminis with regards to duality when we have the same pattern going for us? Every one of us has a dual nature as well; we have positive and negative traits combined. We tend to show off these traits when the situation demands it, but it doesn't change the fact that it is present in all of us.

If we don't talk about the content of this chapter, we will be giving an unbalanced narrative, and astrology is all about striking a balance. Here's a fact for sure, we all love to talk about our positive traits and how nice, charming, hardworking, etc. we are yet shy away from the negative characteristics.

If some persons had some super power, they will only want others to see what they show them, which could be the positives mostly. But life doesn't work that way, and before we get on with the analysis, you should know and embrace certain truths.

Your negative traits are not meant to hold you bound or cause you to feel inadequate. They are flaws that prompt you always to seek improvement and the desire to work hard at building yourself up regardless of the amount of success you enjoy in life.

Imagine if you were perfect with 100% positive traits only. You always have a smile on your face, you don't have interpersonal conflicts with anyone, you are like a ray of sunshine to everyone else, and you are the all-round good man/woman. How do you think your life will be?

Your life will be perfect in your eyes, but ultimately dull!

Negative traits and flaws add some spice into your life because they remind you of your human nature, and they help you make modifications that strengthen your character.

Most of the beautiful things you see and admire had some negative traits in them, but because you don't know the background process you only admire the finished product.

For example, they say "Diamonds are a girl's best friend" so we all love the sparkly jewelry, but diamonds were not always perfect, and they had to go through a lot of polishing to arrive at that state.

As we go through this chapter together, think of yourself as a diamond, you are sparkly and beautiful, but you need those negative traits to shine even more brightly.

Below, you will find your astrological sign with a detailed analysis of your positive and negative traits. Now, remember the aim is not to rub your nose in the sand but to empower you with information about yourself that helps you take proactive steps towards refining your character.

You can also look out for the traits of a romantic partner, close friend, or family member so you can better understand why they act in a certain and what you can do to help them get better.

Ready to unravel the beautiful and exciting aspects of your life? Let's do this!

Aries

Positive

Aries individuals are courageous and enthusiastic; they are willing to face any challenge that comes their way and takes more risks than other signs. They are always striving to be better people with a taste for wonder and adventure.

Their child-like approach towards life makes it possible for them to sip tea and relax even in the face of a huge challenge. They can take up new projects and not be afraid of the outcome.

Negative

Aries are very confrontational, they love to argue, and they are undisciplined. They are insensitive of other people's emotions, and their impulsiveness makes them impatient.

Those born under this sign can be immature and domineering, making friendships with them stressful. When dealing with people, they have issues with they can be rude and disrespectful.

Like stubborn kids, they want everything to go their way, which makes them quite demanding. They can have an emotional outburst creating a scene in public and not be remorseful about it.

Aries is a fire sign, so they are quite emotional, and because of the ram symbol, they are always ready for a fight.

Capricorn

Positive

A Capricorn is a hardworking person who takes his/her life goals seriously and puts in the work to make it happen. They are determined and resourceful, which happens to be fascinating traits of an active person.

Capricorns are ready to wait for as long as it will take for them to achieve their goals because they know that good things take time. Capricorns are also disciplined people who understand the concept of little drops of water, making a mighty ocean. Hence the reason they are very patient.

Before a Capricorn makes a decision, he/she must have all the facts because they are wise people who want to make mature and sensible decisions at all times.

They are not impulsive not even with purchases, and they are very ambitious. When they are under pressure, they are graceful and can fix any bad situation.

Negative

They tend to be shy hence the reason they will prefer to stay home and enjoy their own company or the company of their best pals. They don't easily change their views, making them somewhat stubborn.

They are cold, controlling, and unapproachable because most times they like to be by themselves and unconsciously tell everyone else to back off. Sometimes they exude passivity by not going for what they want; they allow life pass by them.

Before they can trust someone, they need time and must have studied the person thoroughly because they are very distrusting people. The threat of being betrayed is quite palpable to them, and because of this insecurity, they can be very pessimistic about everything.

Due to their commitment to work, their emotions suffer, they would instead take on work at the office than a dinner date if they have to choose, and this makes them detached from others.

They can be self-centered, arrogant, and ruthless in a bid to achieve their set goals.

Taurus

Positive
When you think of someone who will be there for you in your time of need, think about someone under the Taurus sign. When they make a promise to you, they will fulfill it, and they can never be fake friends.

They take their time before making a decision hence the reason they can minimize failures and mistakes. Taurus is also influential people who are willing to use their strength to help other people; they are thoughtful, generous, kind, and resilient (nothing can put them down).

They seek to derive the greatest joy and pleasure from life; hence, the reason they are thrilled people. Another modest trait about them is the fact that they are down to earth (regardless of their success), polite, and delightful.

They are also financially and emotionally independent, making them the best choice of romantic partners. They rarely fail because they are persistent and self-motivated.

Negative
Oh, Taurus are stubborn people, once they know their path and purpose nothing stops them, but it also means that they are sometimes too stubborn to listen to a difference in opinion. They can be very mundane, and if they are not motivated, they will be lazy.

They can be possessive, which makes them jealous enough to become resentful in a relationship. Taurus individuals also have a vile temper, and in the heat of their anger, they can say hurtful words.

When they don't feel like working, they can be lazy and not motivated to do anything which can make them unproductive. Taurus loves to spend money on food, clothes, and other material things that catch their attention.

They are also self-indulgent making them seek a lot of "Me time" even when the people in their lives need their attention.

Gemini

Positive
Geminis are witty, which makes them fascinating people; they are curious; hence, the reason they are full of knowledge. Their enthusiasm is real as they portray a deep love for life and live it to the full.

Geminis have a mixed personality that is adjustable, they don't struggle with expressing their thoughts and emotions, and they are the life of the party.

A very striking trait about Geminis is their ability to relate with anyone they meet; they get along with strangers and everyone else. Their adaptive personality makes it easier for them to live anywhere and with anyone because they are free spirits.

What you will always get with a Gemini is an open, straight forward individual who is versatile, communicative, and friendly. You can feel the warm aura around them from the moment you come in contact with them.

Geminis are also very smart and sharp; they remember aspects of what you say to them, can flow with anyone in a group and have brilliant communicative skills. In some instances they are soft-spoken and some other cases they are outspoken loudly (it's all about the duality of their personality).

Their interest in a wide variety of topics makes them quite versatile, so when you have a conversation with them, you are enthralled by their depth of knowledge.

Negative
Geminis are mainly inconsistent; it is challenging for them to start one thing and stick with it long term. They cannot also make up their mind, so they are faced with an urgent situation where they need to make a decision they stall.

They also tend to take on more than they can do hence the reason they become anxious, especially when a thing doesn't turn out as they expect. Geminis are also shallow; they are quick to start an argument but cannot see it through to the end.

They sometimes lack discipline and direction in their life, which is why most Geminis recognize that they need a mentor who can help them maintain consistency in their lives.

One of their bad habits is the love for gossip, they cannot help, but gossip and they are most likely the ones who start a rumor in the office or someplace else. Geminis have the worst mood swings that come at an unpredictable timing and prevents them from enjoying certain happy moments in their lives.

Pisces

Positive

Some of the positive words you can use to describe a Pisces are imaginative, creative, selfless, and compassionate. They can think outside the box, and they are warm people.

Their ability to use the power of imagination makes them natural artists who can create a masterpiece with art. Compassion is a strong trait they embody; they can sense when someone needs something and will devote themselves to it selflessly until it is done.

They are also opposed to crime and acts of injustice against other people. A typical Pisces is sensitive on the inside; this is a good trait that makes him/her have a high level of emotional intelligence.

Pisces is also the kind of person that can get along with everyone else without trying to exert control or try to influence people to suit their needs. They are kind and gentle towards themselves and others.

Those under the sign are very imaginative, they can think on their toes, they are soft and always in a helpful mood even with strangers. Although their efforts at helping others are not much appreciated as it should be, it doesn't stop them from being consistent with help.

Negative

A major flaw that the Pisces has is the "Escapist mindset" which makes them blame everyone and everything else for their problems except themselves. They are the type of people who will say that their luck or destiny is responsible for their problem.

The extreme idealist who can judge the best efforts of others as too mediocre is the Pisces because they have an idea in their head of what something should be. They are also sensitive; emotional outbursts are a norm for them.

Pessimism is also a negative trait with the Pisces, especially when things do not happen as they would want them to play out. They are lazy with stuff they don't care about.

Most Pisces also try to look for things they can use to aid their escapist mentality as such if you are a Pisces, you need to seek help with this flaw else you can quickly revert to alcohol or drugs as an escapist tool.

A lot of times, they are detached from reality because they are often in their personalized wonderland in their heads. Giving up is always an option for the Pisces, and when they give up, they go right into the imaginary world where they are free from obligation or reality.

They cannot withhold enthusiasm for long, so even with their work, the reason they tend to work hard is if they find that the work is meaningful and aids a cause dear to their heart.

When the Pisces feelings are hurt, he/she takes it personally, and this is a recipe for low self-esteem. Most of the accomplishments they desire to attain do not come to fruition because they have low self-esteem.

They are weak-willed, and when surrounded by stronger signs, their ambition and ideas are easily crushed. Pisces are easily influenced and pressured by others.

Leo

Positive
One of your most observable traits is that you love attention, you are energetic, a born leader, and you hate being bored, which is why you keep yourself surrounded by people and engage in activities.

Leos are charismatic, friendly, and lovable; they are also very ambitious with all aspects of their lives. If there is one trait that makes you stand out, it is the tenacity to succeed at whatever you do.
With Leos, what you see is what you get, they don't have to hide their personalities as they are bold enough to let their pure light shine through everywhere. They will never hesitate to tell you the truth; they are kind to everyone they meet.

Leos are also helpful as they are willing to assist those in need. All Leos are born as people worthy of love, admiration, and praise. Their generosity is also a major strong point for them.

Leos are also optimistic; for them, the glass is half-full and not half-empty, they are loyal and demand the same kind of loyalty they give to others.

Negative
Leos are headstrong people; you will go through a great deal of trouble to convince them to change their minds when they believe in something. They have a big ego as well, so big that it can affect them on their path to success.

Individuals who are Leos are also jealous and possessive; they are dominating because they want to rule over everyone else. Another flaw in them is the fact they are impatient with everything.

Whatever they desire, they want to get, and this can make them self-centered. Some Leos are also pretentious; they don't say what they mean when they need to; instead, they would rather say what helps them remain in the position of power.

Leos are proud, this pride they feel can get in the way of them maintaining their integrity. They are also too proud to admit when an idea they propose doesn't seem right for a situation.

In their workplaces, their dominating aura can make employees or subordinates wary of them. Their love for the spotlight makes them dramatic. Arrogance is a word often used to describe a Leo, instead of saying "Sorry" when they're wrong they will seek out other creative ways to appease the aggrieved individual.

Virgo

Positive
Virgos are talented and intelligent individuals that are great leaders across varying fields. Their thirst for knowledge is a trait that enables that seek higher achievements, and they are always curious about how things work.
Virgos are problem solvers, and most admirably they are modest people, regardless of the extent of success they achieve they will never brag about it or show off.

As a Virgo, you can accomplish whatever you set your mind on, you are reliable and never settle for mediocrity even when other people do the same.

You are gentle, wise, and good at analyzing situations to determine what should be done the right way. People always come to you for advice because you seem to have everything in order in your life.

You can be a perfectionist as well who wants things done right, you don't believe in the fantasy world, and you pay close attention to detail. You are always happy to learn more.

Negative
Because you have an image in your head about how you want things done, you do not accept alternative ideas or

suggestions. You are very critical and fussy because you want things to be perfect.

You are finicky with details which can get you feeling stressed out when details are not well placed for your viewing pleasure. You can be harsh and conservative (no to modern and new ideas), and you are judgmental.

You can be difficult when you want to be because you are never satisfied, as a parent you have high expectations for your kids and when they don't meet such goals you express your disappointment in a harsh way towards them.

Your high level of intelligence can be a turn-off because you don't accept other people the way you accept yourself. Sometimes you see them beneath you when they don't express the same level of perfectionism you embody.

Virgos do not connect to the modern world, they are stuck to conservative ideals in their minds. They are over-demanding of their colleagues, partners and employees.

Scorpio

Positive
You are intensely passionate and tend to make people around you come alive, when you step into a room you light it up and this is what people refer to as positive energy. Your determination puts you on the verge of success all the time as this matches our ambition.

You always get things done and you are highly intuitive which makes it harder for people to deceive you. You are a brave and focused individual who is motivated internally, and you know what you want out of life.

Your instincts are your most valuable traits as you always know who to trust and who to avoid making you have a strong inner circle of friends you can rely on any day.

You don't like it when things become a routine, and it is because you are a passionate individual. You can analyze people and see them for who they are, and this helps to become a good leader over others.

The trait that helps you succeed in life easily is that of ambition, you are motivated by money, position and power. You will always stand by those you love when they are faced with difficulties, and you deliver on your promises.

You make the best out of every situation when it is a daunting challenge; you are also not easily diverted from your path and life purpose.

Negative
Scorpios are known for being possessive and jealous because they can read people's minds, and they don't trust easily. They can be deeply hurt when treated unfairly, and they love to dominate every situation even in their relationships.

They tend to be suspicious of everyone, fearful of what people can do to them and very manipulative. If plans don't go the way they anticipated, they become angry. When people try to stand up for themselves instead of being manipulated by them, they get frustrated.

In relationships, Scorpios do not care about what the partners want most of the time, so they try to impose their desires on wishes on the other person.

They are also jealous of relationships which could translate into loyalty on their part, but if left unchecked can lead to problems. You can be strong-headed and become obsessed with people and things quickly.

They can hold a grudge for years and find it difficult to forgive when betrayed. They tend to be vengeful, and when they lose their temper, no one can calm them down.

Sagittarius

Positive
You are an optimistic person who loves to have fun, and people love having you around. Your versatility and curiosity make it natural for you to rattle about anything that interests you.

Sagittarius are full of energy which they use to travel the world and your sense of independence is one of the best things about you. Your happiness isn't determined by what others say or do as you have a good sense of judgment to know what is right and wrong for you.

Your honest nature is a breath of fresh air as you are quick to speak your mind, never trying to hide your true feelings and say what you think about a situation.

You are friendly with an open –mind, interested in people and can strike up a conversation with anyone, which means you are bold. You have a massive heart which makes you a very generous person.

When people spend time conversing with you, they are easily impressed by your wit and ability to contribute to the discourse even when it is about something you are not familiar with.

Negative
Your careless nature enables you to take things for granted, sometimes you take the honesty trait a bit too far, sharing your opinions when it isn't solicited, and this can cause friction in your relationships.

You are impatient, inconsistent especially with things that are difficult and you are overconfident with a grand idea of yourself and abilities. You can be very loud and unwilling to let others speak.

You lack empathy skills because you lack awareness of the impact your words have on people, so you claim to "Say it as it is" but in the real sense, you are saying it as it suits you without considering how it affects the other person.
There are times people want a sugar-coated response; they can never get it from you. Boredom occurs too quickly with you, and you tend to change activities as soon as you start feeling overwhelmed by them.

You hate responsibilities at work and in your relationships because you are mostly laid-back. You think you are so perfect and cannot be consistent at something long-term.

Cancer

Positive
You are empathetic hence the reason you care so much about other people. You have a nurturing personality that is loving and patient; in fact, this is what you are known for mostly: caring for people.

You also know how to take care of yourself, which enables you to spend time doing the things you love. You are creative and inventive with ideas; you understand the language of emotions and can be extremely sensitive.

You are in touch with yourself, and can channel your emotions positively, put you enjoy emotional stability. You are also a very supportive friend who is always there for the family.

When the people in your life think about you, they think of a solid rock which is a pillar in their lives. You are also very protective and faithful to others, never expecting anything in return for your acts of kindness.

You always present brilliant ideas when amid other people and you rely heavily on your intuition to make decisions.

Negative
Sometimes you feel overwhelmed by your compassion for others, and it can make you seem distant and icy emotionally. This overwhelming feeling to help others also makes you experience mood swings.

You tend to be pessimistic sometimes and swift to drop projects if you feel like they wouldn't work out. You exhibit clinginess through your unwillingness to move on when things come to an abrupt end (relationships, work, etc.).

You are also overly emotional with a lot of imaginary setbacks that cause you to be suspicious of everyone; fear is a constant companion for you.
When you are in your worst mood, you can withdraw from people and become uncommunicative, which only further buttresses the fact that you let your emotions get the better of you. Your feelings prompt you to make poor judgment and this is a trait that makes you miss out on opportunities.

Your heightened level of pessimism makes it difficult for you to have successful long-term relationships or careers. You also have trust issues with people because you are vulnerable and want to be sure no one is taking advantage of you.

If your overly emotional state is left unchecked, it can lead to depression, making others uncomfortable around you. You are easily carried away by negative emotions rather than the positive ones.

Libra

Positive
What's not to love about a Libra? You are incredibly charming with the most interesting personality. You are also very courteous even in your conversations as you speak with charisma wherever you are with other people.

Libras are often described as cool-headed people who enjoy partnerships with others and strive to maintain peace in their relationships. They can be diplomatic when faced with a crisis they need to resolve.

They would take the time to listen to all parties involved in the issue with a great deal of patience, hence the reason they are the ideal persons for conflict resolution.

If anyone wants to get anything done, you are the go-to person. The influence of Venus as your ruling planet makes you romantic with excellent manners that are pleasing.

You love fairness and will only stick with an idea if you think it is just and true. Your sensitive nature also makes you a good listener.

Negative
Laziness and indecision are two flaws you embody; you might be inspired to do something this minute and change your mind in an instant. Then you never come back to it again. You also tend to overthink things, thus making you unproductive in the long run. You have a fickle personality that lacks substance; hence, the reason you make promises you cannot keep.

You are easily impressed by what people show you on the outside while forgetting to pay attention to the inner traits. Because you have a charming personality, it makes you pretend to be pleasant even when you are not in the mood for pleasantries.

When faced with a tough situation that requires your input, you become indecisive and would instead pass on the task to someone else than deal with your indecision.

If Libras are not mindful of their character, the negative aspects can get the better part of the positive traits, so don't stop working on the refinement of your traits.

Aquarius

Positive
You are an amiable person this is what you are most known for (being popular amongst friends). You also try your best to make the world better than you met it as your full range of interest also makes you a very creative person.

You are great with finances because you are entirely independent and an amazing characteristic about you is the fact that you keep your word. In today's world, finding people who keep their word is an arduous task, so you are great with that.

You tolerate others due to your friendly nature, and you are a highly intellectual individual admired by a lot of people. To top off the positive traits, you are a great listener!

Negative
You tend to be sporadic hence not having structures in your life as you bounce off from one passion to the next one almost immediately. You can be very unpredictable, which can make you appear stubborn to some others.

Your "Know it all" attitude prevents you from learning new ideas and concepts from other people. Your dedication to a task is primarily determined by your mood, which is inconsistent.

Sometimes for no particular reason, you can become distant from friends and family members, preferring to stay detached until you get into a good mood again.

Another worrisome trait is the fact that you have an "All or nothing" approach towards life, which makes you impatient. You prefer to either have what you need or have nothing at all.

You are a complete human being, and you are special because you've got a mix of the good traits you can retain and the bad features you need to work on to get better. Don't stop making improvements and continually add some value to your life by doing better every day.

Some persons erroneously "Settle" for the traits they have; they accept the characteristics that are not so pleasant and would do nothing to make it better. Remember that these details were shared with you so you can do something positive with the information.

Life is what you make of it and not what you settle for while avoiding the "Perfectionist" idea; you can also be someone who is known as a "Work in progress."

Every day presents an opportunity for you to make better decisions with your life. After reading through the concluding section of this book, come back to this chapter and start seeking ways through which you can strike a balance with your character.

Some other persons are not privy to this information; they don't understand why they are impatient or a bit harsh towards people. But you have access to this information, which means you have all the tools required to transform how you view yourself and the relationship you have with others.

Having this kind of information also means you can help others to discover more about their purpose in life and the path they should take.

So in the next chapter, you will learn how you can take control of your life's path and purpose, sounds exciting right? Flip over and get right to it.

Chapter Six
How To Take Control of Your Life Path & Purpose

Astrology is about discovery; you will always learn something new or discover something about yourself that makes life even more meaningful, which is the reason why the concept of control is so important.

Are you in control of your life at this moment?

You don't have to answer the question in a hurry, take your time to think about it for a few minutes.

If you think that you are in control, what parameters did you use to arrive at your answer?

We all like to think we are in control, it's only natural to want to believe that about ourselves, but we must be sure about this because it isn't about how you feel but about the reality of the situation.

A lot of times, we hand over the reins of our lives when we allow ourselves to become influenced by others or when we absorb someone else's beliefs about life and make it our own.

We lose control when our partners call all the shots, and we compromise on speaking up and experiencing our sun sign for the "Sake of peace" in a relationship. Even in the workplace, we don't maintain consistency of character because we are only focused on impressing the boss and colleagues.

There are several instances of how people lose their path in life and give up control, and you may have even given up authority subconsciously without knowing it.

We mentioned earlier that astrology is about discovery, but it gets better, discovery aims to equip you with the right information skillset that enables you to live life to the fullest potential.

The concepts below will help you take control of your life's path and purpose while empowering you to be the best version of yourself that you can be even now.

Achieve Emotional Stability

We are going to talk about changing your thinking in a moment, but before we get there you should know that emotional balance is a must!

Control is about being in charge of your life, and it all begins with how you feel. How are you feeling right now? Do you tend to have emotional outbursts when you feel overwhelmed? We have all been there, that moment when you feel like your emotions have taken over and you wished you had better control.

For some astrological signs, emotional stability can be a massive challenge because of the way their personalities are wired. For example, an individual who is under the Capricorn sign may be prone to feeling depressed because he/she is a high achiever who wants to win at all times.

So when the tides change, and it seems like there will be no wins the person quickly becomes frustrated which could lead to emotional outbursts and other outward display of anger that doesn't send a positive message across to others about his/her personality.

But your astrological sign shouldn't be an excuse for a lack of control, yes it is a factor but you can build on it and become better by learning how to be emotionally stable.

Giving room for emotional imbalance will make it easier for you to lose yourself, you will discover that you no longer make rational decisions and your whole life is based on how you FEEL and not what is REAL.

It has been said repeatedly in this book that the purpose of sharing and teaching you astrological concepts is to empower you, to help you know what you can do with the information the universe gives you.

Whatever you learn about yourself will help you gain better control of yourself, and this includes achieving emotional stability. You will never always be in a perfect place so get ready to handle your emotions when they come at you by maintaining the same emotional state through good and bad times.

Change Your Thinking

The way you think affects the level of control you exert over your life, let me ask you this question, do you ever think about what you are thinking about?

I know it sounds a bit complicated, but it is a vital question we often never ask ourselves. Thousands of thoughts go through our minds daily, and if we are not keen on being conscious about what we are thinking about, we will absorb the wrong ideas every minute.

Astrology helps you look beyond what you are thinking and makes you wonder why you have that thought process in the first place. All we will talk about in this chapter about control will be ultimately linked to your thought process, so please take this idea seriously.

Now there are several layers to a person's thought processes; thoughts do not just spring forth; they are products of experiences, activities, dreams, conversations, and so many other things.

Sometimes the thoughts come all at once, and your mind is filled, which can be overwhelming, at those points, you shouldn't be wondering about the idea itself but what motivated the thought.

The things that make you think about what you think about is the real problem.

So let us assume you keep thinking about not being good enough at work and it cripples you on the inside. You check your astrological chart, and it tells you otherwise, but you can't shake the feeling off.

Which means you need to deal with the underlying factors that prompted the feeling of being inadequate. Did you have a hard time at school? Have you been struggling with succeeding lately?

Taking control means you will have to deal with these back end issues so you can live freely. Change your self-talk, modify the language you use as your inner voice, and let your thoughts only reflect the great expectations you have about your life.

Compartmentalize Your Relationships

This is the step you take when you realize that your relationships are now getting the better part of you and you need to step back to reevaluate the situation.

One of the main reasons why you discover astrology is so you can consider the relationship you have with others and the kind of influence they have over you.

But this doesn't mean that your life has to be an open book for everyone to come in and cross boundaries as they will. So what can you do, compartmentalize your relationship!
In your kitchen, regardless of how disorganized it may be, utensils cannot be inside the microwave and eggs cannot be inside the sink. Everything has a place, everything is compartmentalized and so long the things in the kitchen stay the same; you wouldn't look for anything when you need it.

The concept of compartmentalizing your relationships is a way of placing everyone in your life exactly where they should be, so they have defined boundaries. A person who doesn't put people in compartments will lose control over his/her life.

There is a place for best friends in your life; there is also a place for colleagues, family members, romantic partners, etc. your husband/wife shouldn't have any influence over the decisions you make at work.

Your best friend has no business telling you how to live with your partner, and you shouldn't be compelled to attend a beach party because your colleague is assuming you are both best friends.

So compartmentalizing your relationships enables you to create mental boundaries that manifest in the physical with your contacts which also empowers you to take better control of your life.

Avoid Distracting Negative Influences

The reason you may feel like you don't have a lot of control over your life is that you have given too much attention to those who influence you negatively. We discussed extensively on negative and positive traits from a personal perspective in the previous chapter.

Here, we are not looking at the concept of negativity as it applies to you inwardly but how it applies you outwardly. One bad apple spoils the whole bunch and that one negative influence in your life can completely corrupt your mental and physical space.

We unknowingly give toxic people the power to control our thoughts, behavior, and feelings, which is a clear indication that you are losing control. Truthfully, you will never discover your purpose when you are always surrounded by negative energy.

The first question you should ask yourself is, who am I around most of the time? Take note of the people you are most associated with and monitor the influence they have over your life.

What are your associations doing to you? What do they have me doing? What are they feeding me with mentally? What have they got me reading? What do they make me say?

Some friends are complainers; they never see anything good in any situation. When you all hang out they complain about the weather, the waiter, the food, the ambiance at the restaurant, their entire existence is steeped in complaints.

If you have such people in your life, flee!

Listen to everything you have learned here is meant to make YOU a better person, not the person next to you, but YOU! You can only become as good as the people around you.

Disassociation is never an easy decision, but in some cases, it is essential. I am not suggesting that you cut the person entirely at first. You can do it systematically until the person(s) gradually eases out of your life.

After disassociating yourself from such person, take the time to expand your associations with the right kind of people. Find successful people who align with your purpose and make them a part of your life.

By successful people, we are not only talking about those who are financially well off, but those who have discovered themselves, positive people who add value to your life and you do the same for them.

With negative influences out of your life, you can take control of your path and be the best version of yourself. Do not tolerate negative impacts because they are long-term friends or family members.

The duration of the relationship doesn't matter because at this moment you are well equipped to handle your life, and if you have to take on this path alone, it will be worth it.

What do you think?

Isn't it better to walk alone than walk with the weight of negative influences in your life? You probably know the answer, and it means you are on track to taking control of your life.

Meditation

Lao Tzu once said that "If you correct your mind, the rest of your life will fall into place."

In taking control of your life and your purpose, you will need to take control of your mind first. The content of your mind will reflect in everything you do, which is why meditation is crucial.

Through constant meditation, you will realize an actual act, that happiness cannot be bought or derived from your accomplishments; it is a product of how you feel on the inside. But how will you know your inner feelings when you are not in constant touch with your mind?

We live in a fast world with fast food, fast cars, fast internet, and amid the speed we hand over the reins of our life to systems that have been built to make you lose control.

Examples of such systems are social media app, games, and other distracting activities that make you focus on everything else but yourself. Meditation is the calm in the storm; it is the one activity you can engage in that keeps you focused on your path and purpose.

The start of your day largely determines how the remaining parts of the day will do, and meditation gives you a great start. If you have a great start every morning for the rest of your life, think about the positive impact it will have on your life long-term.

Meditation also enables you to generate and project loving energy from the universe which you can use to become compassionate to yourself, friends, family, and sometimes strangers.

All you need in a day is one hour of meditation, and you will have access to the positive energy you take with you everyone you go. With this attribute of meditation, you will not be a dumping ground for someone else's negative vibes; you will create your aura that permeates every fiber of your being.

How does a person take control of his/her life without being self-confident? It isn't possible meditation increases self-confidence because when you are always in that state of self-awareness, you realize that you are enough.

You love yourself (positive and negative traits), and you are not bothered about what other people think about you. Looking at the world and yourself through positive lenses increases self-confidence, it makes you feel like you don't have to "Fit" in because you were made to stand out.

Be Intentional About Everything
An intentional person is a calculative one who is also in control most of the time, such a person isn't moved by circumstances and does what he/she sets out to do regardless of what may happen.

There are times when you will need to be spontaneous, the truth is, you will know when such a time comes, and it wouldn't have to be severe aspects of life. But mostly, you must become conscious of being intentional; that's the keyword right there "Conscious."

When you are aware of it, you set out to do what you want to do and not what society expects. It all begins with the small decisions that will build up to become a massive part of your life.

Here is an illustration to buttress the point.

If you studied chapter four intensively and you realized your financial status based on your astrological chart, you will know the kind of financial decisions you ought to make at every point in your life.

So if you are not the right place financially, you will need to check the kind of purchases you make and monitor your monetary decisions. An intentional person will go on

Amazon to search for a specific product that he/she requires, make a purchase, and leave the store.

But an unintentional person who is fully aware of his/her financial inconsistency will get on Amazon to buy an item, make a purchase and instead of leaving the online platform, he/she stays on looking for other irrelevant things that are not within his/her price range.

Maybe it's a new summer bag or a new laptop someone else owns; they make an additional two purchases they can't afford, waste time window shopping and at the end of the day they have to deal with the consequences of being impulsive.

The illustration above is a typical scenario of a person who is not in control of his/her life. This individual is controlled by something else (a desire to be like other people), and this is not the reason you learned so much about astrology.

While there is nothing wrong with making more purchases if you chose to, it becomes a problem when you are not intentional about it becomes it shows a lack of control. The reason you received information on your finances in relation with astrology is so you can make better decisions that are guided by facts.

When you're overly impetuous, it slowly builds up to become a habit, you might think that you are only making small purchases on Amazon but when you look at the $10 or $15 you carelessly spent each day, you will realize that when put together, it would have been put to good use.

The ability for you to take control of your life through intentionality doesn't relate solely with finances; it cuts across all areas of your life. Take some off reading for a few minutes and think about the aspects of your life you will need to be much more intentional about.

Moments of self-reflection helps us see ourselves from the eyes of the universe, what is it saying to you? Are you intentional with your life and decisions?

Be True to Yourself

The importance of staying true to yourself cannot be overemphasized, especially within the ambit of astrology. Regardless of how close you are to a person (even if the individual is your twin), you can never use his/her birth chart for your astrological predictions.

This shows the extent of uniqueness you enjoy as a person as such if you are going to take charge of your life and control your path, you must be true to yourself.

When you start sacrificing your identity for other people, that's when you know you are no longer an authentic person. So firstly, do not sacrifice your integrity for anyone (not even the person you are in a relationship with).

People can have opinions about your life, but it isn't your responsibility to implement every suggestion or accept every comment made about you. Now you know who you are through the astrological details shared about you, uphold your peculiar nature, and stay true to your personality.

More so, learn to set strict boundaries in your lie regarding your time and space. A lot of people lose control over their lives by giving access to everyone with their time and space.

Listen to this, you are not a slice of pizza, and you are not responsible for everyone else's happiness, you cannot make everyone happy which is why you need to create boundaries in your life especially with your time.

Don't show up for that event just because your friend will be upset if you don't attend if you are unable to go because you are doing some other personal things that are self-fulfilling then decline the invitation politely.

Don't accept people's needy behavior because you are trying to be understanding; we are talking about your life here, you should be the only one who has a say on how your time is spent and the places you go.

More importantly, do not feel obligated to care about the same things someone else cares about, you will be relinquishing your power when you do that. Acknowledge that you love what you love and you don't need to endorse what someone else likes to show support for them.

A vital part of being true to yourself is saying what you mean, which is an indication that you're a person of integrity. There is a lot of societal and peer pressure on people to repeat the opinions of others.

But as a person who is true to his/herself, you need to resist this societal norm by allowing your genuine thoughts and feelings shine through in all sincerity and humility.

Over time you will be known as someone who doesn't compromise on integrity and people will respect you for it. Those who are not true to themselves strive to be "Liked," hence the reason they become people pleasers.

Don't struggle to be liked; instead, strive to be respected!

Respect only comes to those who know who they are and are willing to stand by their truth even if they stand alone. Astrology has empowered you with information about yourself, hold on to it, and use it to exert control over your life.

A wise man once said that you could lose everything materially dear to you in the world and you will be okay eventually, but if you lose yourself, you have lost it all. We have learned so much, and we are still learning, the details of this chapter yet will determine if you will utilize what you've learned or not.

Ensure that you are always in control of your life through your thoughts, being intentional, avoiding the pitfalls of negative influences and mental exercises such as meditation.

What's next after this lesson? Is it possible to translate all you've learned about astrology into an applicable life process? Don't bother thinking about the answers; the next chapter has all the details.

Chapter Seven
What's Next In Your Life?

The question above is a recurring one we ask all through our lives when we conquer one stage and seek out the next. Human beings are built to seek more, so a baby is born, the parents are excited and the "What's next?" narrative begins. Now we have this baby when will he start to crawl? The baby crawls, and we are excited, then we wonder when he/she will walk?

The baby walks and excitement soars, next we think when this baby be ready for school? So you see that expectations never end and it is the same with knowledge on astrology. We have been on this journey from learning the basics of astrology to unraveling other exciting aspects of the idea, but now we are at the last stop of this journey asking what's next?

The answer to the question lies in one word, usefulness!

When you graduate from college, the "What next question" means how are you going to add value to society with what you've learned and that's what we will do with astrology in this section.

As mentioned earlier on, astrology is all around us, but it can only become visible to those who use it. We didn't talk about your career, finances, and relationships just so you can read, the previous sections all prepared you for this moment.

Generally, whatever you learn in life should become useful to you in real-time, so even outside of astrology, you should be intentional about the impact certain information have in your life. Is it helpful? Will it change situations for you? This is so important hence the reason an entire chapter is dedicated to it. Until you start practicing what you know, you know nothing!

In this section, you will discover ways through which you can apply astrology to your life and make the experience palpable enough for long-term results. Since we are dealing with the concept of usefulness, you should know that this section is also a practical one that will require you to take action as you read.

Strengthen Your Inner Voice (Instinct)

We all have that voice within us that directs our actions, but sometimes some people say that they feel conflicted with they hear the voice. The reason they think this way is because they haven't empowered their instinct using astrology.

Here is how it works.

With astrology, you get to learn more about yourself which leads to self- awareness, this feeling of being aware will cause you to feed your mind with the right kind of information based on what you've discovered through astrology.

So you will be reshaping your inner voice to suit the reality of your personality such that when you are faced with a situation, you know what to do and your instincts are correct rather than conflicted.

The reason you felt a bit of confusion in the past is that you didn't have a firm grasp over your personality, well now you do, and now you know what astrology can do for you. Use it to empower that inner voice, so you are neither lost nor confused about life.

Tool for Self-Awareness/Discovery

Have you ever played poker? If you have, you will agree that it is quite impossible to win at a game if you don't know the cards in your possession. Likewise, you cannot succeed in life if you don't have an accurate idea of who you are.

Self-awareness is so critical in today's world where we are encouraged to be like other people. Astrology enables you to know yourself and have a deeper connection with your personality.

It can be challenging for anyone to be completely objective about themselves, we are emotional creatures, so even when the truth about us stares us in the face, we fail to acknowledge it.

Through astrology, your personality is presented to you in the most objective way, which will be useful when you need to make individual life-changing decisions.

With astrology, you get an unfiltered version of who you and this is something you don't get on social media or even with your friends. People will always say what you want to hear, and if you listen to them long enough, you will lose yourself.

The next thing for you with astrology is to use it as a tool for self-discovery such that you know your values, and you are not willing to compromise them for anything or anyone.

Self-discovery is often the first step you take on the astrological journey; it is the reason it was presented to you in the earliest chapters because it is very crucial. All the times you spent reading through newspapers searching for astrological signs, you were trying to find yourself.

When you know yourself, the world will not tell you to conform to its standards; you wouldn't settle for any relationship because you are desperate. You will be patient with yourself and learn to trust your incredible journey through life.

Build Compassion Towards Others

When we asked the question "What next?" at the start of this chapter, it wasn't a question solely meant for what you could do for yourself but what you can do for others as well.

It is effortless to become self-absorb when you start discovering things about yourself through astrology. At such moments you feel like you know so much about yourself and you are in control of what happens.

While it is great that you are learning this much about yourself, you must also realize that if your relationships are not reflecting this functional space, you are in right now, there will be problems.

Compassion is akin to being emotionally intelligent; astrology helps you become compassionate when you discover the reasons certain people behave the way they do.

We dedicated an amount of time to connect the dots between you and your relationships in this book because that is what astrology is about (a link between you, the universe, and others).

If you are a leader in your organization, by learning more about the astrological signs of your subordinates, you will be kinder and much more understanding knowing that they behave in a certain way because it's who they are.

If you are in a relationship or married, the issues you have with your partner will no longer cause friction between the both of you because you have an understanding of this other person's weakness and you are compassionate towards them.

Sometimes you don't even need to know a person for an extended period to understand them, by just knowing their Sun sign you can tell much more about them which makes your interactions more detailed and laced with compassion when required.

In individual relationships, you may feel like your partner is trying to manipulate you, so this puts you on guard all the time. When there is a minor argument, you take it to the extreme because you want to avoid being manipulated.

But what you term "Manipulation" might be a manifestation of your partner's sign through his/her personality. If your partner is a Leo, for instance, he/she is a born leader. Leos are bold (they are often referred to as lions), and we all know the lion is an intimidating animal.

So your partner is merely exhibiting the natural traits of his/her sign, and when you get to understand this, you will not only be compassionate, you will also start to enjoy your relationship.

This same idea applies to the concept of being judgmental towards other people. We tend to pass judgment when we don't understand a person, so it's easier to label the individual based on what they did.

Astrology enables you to go beyond considering a person solely on what they do but also on who they are. You will be more patient, tolerating, and kinder to people when you start using your astrological knowledge.

Practical Guide Into Your Strengths & Weaknesses

What's next for you with astrology? You can use the knowledge gained to gain insight into your strengths and weaknesses, which is a significant indicator for a grand or tiring life.

We often struggle with certain key things in life because we don't know what we are good at and what we should outsource to someone else, this ignorance makes us want to do everything, and eventually we end up doing nothing.

Do you recall the example we mentioned at the beginning of this chapter about graduating from college? Well, when you go to college you cannot study everything, regardless of your IQ level, you can only settle for one course or at most a double major.

The reason for this is because when you settle for one course, you will be concentrating on your strength and harnessing the power of your abilities. Which also means that you will most likely struggle if you end up with a course of study you are not good at.

The brief explanation above using the college situation as a case study is a way of showing you another angle to the usefulness of astrology in your life. When you know your strength, you know what to concentrate on long-term that you can build up to become proficient at it.

Knowledge of your weaknesses will also help you know the areas you need to work on so you can try to achieve a balance. If writing is a core strength for you based on your star, you can intentionally work on that skill, knowing that unlike those who are not "Born writers," you will have an edge.

Before we go further, it is crucial to point out the fact that having the strength or being born with something unique doesn't mean you will attain instant success. You've got to work at it like you don't have the advantage from the universe.

If you remain laid-back about it, someone else who doesn't have the backing of the universe with that skill but works hard at it will surely do better than you. Astrology enables you to spot these personalized features, so you become aware of and work on them.

For your weaknesses or flaws, don't get the information about them and do nothing about it. Some people say "Well based on my star sign I am not a good organizer, so that's the reason my home is in disarray," such a statement only portrays the individual as being laid back and lazy.

Astrology doesn't show you your weaknesses, so you ACCEPT them and do nothing! You are given such information to make your life better; this entire book is about that (making your better).

So even information such as "Weaknesses" should be used productively. Get to know your weaknesses and find ways of getting better with them. You don't have "Organizer" in your charts, but you can make an effort with your home, so do that and life will be exceptional.

Useful for Career Guidance

We spend so much time in life trying to find purpose with our career, wanting to know what we should do that will give us meaning and astrology is useful in that area.

With astrology, you will gain insight into the best choices and career path that will be perfect for you and what is in line with your predictions from the universe.

Although we are always torn between the need to do what we love and what pays the bills, astrology can help you settle for the right option because you will get to do what you are at peace with considering the predictions by the universe.

So we often know deep down within our hearts what we want to do career-wise, but we need that little push or prompting that helps us embrace our inner desires and make them real.

Often you will realize that the deep longing you feel within you of a career you love is what is actually on your cards based on an astrological reading. So astrology can be said to be an idea that helps place you on the right track with your career.

In the second chapter of this book, we presented a detailed insight into the various zodiac signs and a personalized idea on how you are based on your birth chart. So when you go back to that chapter and look at your personality, you will be inspired to make career choices that suit your personality.

Listen, a lot of people end up with jobs they hate not because the job itself isn't good enough but because the offer isn't a suitable match for their personality.

This makes every day with that career, business, or job a challenge, they are not inspired, and they detest Mondays even more than the rest of us. But then there's this other individual who takes the time to unearth what is right for him/her and work seems like a breeze for that person. You need to know that what you have discovered about astrology can transform your life, but you've got to use it to feel the effect of that transformation.

If you are already in a career fix, it isn't too late to pull yourself out of it. Go back to your chart, spend some time getting to know who you are and make career decisions based on what you uncover.

In a world where so many people are driven by money, popularity, and fame, you can find peace with what you do by making such decisions based on what is your chart and what you love to do.

For example, those in the Aries sign are known to be brave risk-takers who are daring; this makes them the most likely sign that will do better with entrepreneurship. They are not afraid to disrupt systems or break the norms.

On the flip side, some persons in the Aries sign might choose to settle for a regular job and become the most valuable in the company because they are bold with their ideas and suggestions if such a person decides to strike out on his/her own (if the charts give such reading) there is hope for massive success.

Be Prepared For Tough Times

Another way through which you can use astrology in real-time is to get prepared for tough times, which are inevitable in life. Astrology gives you a timeframe for specific issues you may face so you will know the problem timeline and be better prepared to handle it.

If you are a Capricorn (for example), you will find that when you use astrology to discover certain things about yourself, you will also get to know the times of the year when you will be faced with stifling problems.

Now the reason for this information isn't to scare you or make you feel like life is unfair; it is just to keep you abreast with an aspect of your life that is real. Problems will always come; it is the same way you breathe; it is part of the life cycle.

But the difference between you and the person who doesn't use astrology is the fact that this other person will have the carpet pulled from under him/her. Things will take a turn for the worse, and they will feel overwhelmed.

When there is a hurricane threat, people are notified, not so they feel scared, but so they can set their homes in order, get their kids off school and be ready for the storm coming their way.

When the hard times dissipate, you will realize that you handled it way better than you expected. So astrology helps you manage the outcomes of certain events that will happen to you.

Another idea you should know is the fact that astrology helps you handle problems productively. Not all issues should be treated with fear and trepidation else you will never make a productive headway with the matter.

Now, with astrology, you will not only learn when problem looms you will get a timing which means that within that timeline you can strategize on how you are going to handle it and still make it work despite the challenge.

This is how you deal with a problem productively; you know that there is a problem, but you are still on the lookout for positive outlets that will cushion the effect of the problem on you mentally and otherwise.

You cannot avert a hurricane, you may not be able to save your home, but you can protect your family and other valuables, so you are not grossly affected.

This is a fantastic way to use what you've learned about astrology; you are not only prepared for the tough times you are optimistically and productively empowered to deal with the issue.

Insight Into The Future

In the course of writing this book, I took the liberty of reaching out to a wide array of individuals who have never used nor believe in astrology; I wanted to know if they would feel better knowing what could happen to them in the coming weeks or years. A more significant percentage of them said life would be much easier to navigate if they had such access.

Astrology has been likened to genetics; when you look at the parents of a child, you can quickly tell how that child will be in certain areas of life. When you practice astrology or consider it, you will gain insight into the future.

Having access to information about what could happen tomorrow today gives you an edge and the advantage, it helps you develop a stricter mindset that keeps you stable even when you know problem approaches.

There is power in optimism, and when you know what the future holds for you, you tend to become optimistic about it. So what's next with astrology for you/ use it to ascertain what the future holds for you and take decisive steps that will bring those events to fruition.

In some cases, your actions (consciously or unconsciously) may cause you to miss a step with what the future has in store for you, it may wait, but it will inevitably happen. Using astrology this way will also help you live life "Prepared" or both the good and the bad.

When something unpleasant happens to us after dealing with the initial shock, we sometimes wish we had a heads-up, something, maybe a word, a feeling that will give us an idea of what is to come.

Get to read your astrological chart often, if you need an astrologer's help get it done and consistently try to look into the future so the steps you take now are aligned into what the future holds. It's akin to making the astrological predictions happen in real-time and even faster.

Why do we have a section for the weather forecast in the news? Have you ever wondered why there is always a weatherman/woman with the news on television? It is because when people know the state of the weather, they are better PREPARED the following day. So they go out with their umbrellas, raincoats and even schedule meetings around that weather forecast, making them get the better of the day regardless of the state of the weather.

The person who didn't get the weather forecast will not have the same story because they weren't prepared. With astrology, you can be ready for the future, and you can make those predictions real seven now.

A person who knows a lot about astrology, in theory, has done well, he/she will be an information expert, but a person who has experiential knowledge will have a much more unique experience because experience trumps knowledge any day and any time.

You are furnished with theoretical knowledge, and it has been a worthwhile experience, but only you can take on the experiential side of this journey. However, when someone asks you, "What's next?" after reading so much about astrology, you will have an answer because, through the content of this chapter, you know what to do!

What a journey!

We are at the end of it already, but there is one more section you must read through that will strengthen you through the process of usefulness, flip over to the concluding section to unravel a crucial idea.

Conclusion

Life is beautiful!

We often feel the pressures of life when we don't take time to discover what the universe has in store for us, so we take on this journey thinking we can do it all and get stuck along the way. The objective of this book is to help you strike a connection between your life and astrology, and we have achieved more than that thus far.

Don't try to walk alone when you can get help from the supreme universe through the concept of astrology, don't try to "Take a guess" at what will work or fail all on your own when you have a system that perfectly aligns your emotions, feelings, thoughts, and circumstances together.

Astrology empowers you to take the reins of your life and tackle your own journey with the assurance of getting impressive results. This has been an inspiring journey thus but there is a crucial concept we must discuss as we round off, it borders on the idea of sustainability.

Information on astrology is replete all over the internet, books, podcasts, etc. with the comprehensive details you've received through this book (as will other people) one can only wonder why people still make the same relationship, financial and life mistakes that they experience.

The reason for their inability to translate what they learn into their lives is because they lack a sustainable approach to learning. After putting this book down so many people will get excited and try out the astrology for a few days, okay maybe a few weeks and then boom! They completely forget about it!

Two years down the road, they will hear someone speak of the positive effect of astrology, and they will say "Oh I used to practice that but not anymore" this is not the way to go when knowledge is acquired. There are three things you should note:

1. *Learning*
2. *Doing*
3. *Sustaining*

So you just completed the first step, you've learned so much about astrology, but you must take the next level by actually doing something with what you've learned. After that, you should start thinking about sustaining it all long-term because that is how it will become a part of your life.

Astrology is not a passive idea, and when you don't take action with it, you will be depriving yourself of the opportunity to add value to your life through the lessons learned.

As we round off this experience here, get excited about the idea of sustainability by actively taking steps towards using astrology in your unique experience. The words in this book should transcend the pages and come alive with your finances, relationships, friendships and every other area of your life.

The question you should be asking yourself at this point is "What am I going to do with the vital lessons gained?" use it, continue with it and let your astrological success story inspires others to do the same.

It's a whole new world now as you harness the potentials of astrology and bask in the feeling of taking control of your life. Ready to strike a secure connection with the universe?

Start implementing, take action, and enjoy the process!

Best Wishes

Sofia Visconti

Numerology:

Discover The Meaning Behind The Numbers in Your Life & Their Secrets to Success, Wealth, Fortune Telling & Happiness

Table of Contents

Introduction

Chapter 1: The History of Numerology

Chapter 2: Methods

Chapter 3: The Meaning of Numbers In Numerology and How Numbers Work

Chapter 4: Getting Started With Numerology / Discovering Your Personal Numerology Blueprint

Chapter 5: Your Birthday Number

Chapter 6: Reveal the Underlying Meaning Behind the Numbers in your Life

Chapter 7: Guidance Regarding Property

Chapter 8: Having a Perfect Relationship with the Knowledge of Numerology

Chapter 9: Establish Your Business Based On Your Lucky Number

Chapter 10: In popular Culture

Conclusion

References

A SPIRITUAL START!

Introduction

"Wow! Wow!! Wow!!!"

These were my words when I first began to have insight into the mystery behind the numbers in my life. I had always thought various events that had an uncanny connection to my Life Path Number were nothing but "coincidences." I used to dismiss numerology as a "pseudoscience" only meant for deluded people, but I know better now. It is interesting to note that as much as people feel the knowledge of numerology is elusive, it is actually all around us. If you had been paying more attention to details, you would have realized that these "secrets" have always been staring you in the face, but you never noticed.

In the Harry Potter story, the favorite subject of Hermione Granger is arithmancy. This subject involves the study of the magical attributes of numbers. Hermione used complex magical charts to predict future events with numbers in the story. Arithmancy is numerology in the real world. According to numerologists, numbers carry immense powers and can give you insight into your personality and capabilities. I say "Congratulations" to you if you are new to numerology because you have been able to come this far.

I am sure that you have chosen to read this book, not out of mere curiosity, but because you want to have a better understanding of yourself. I am convinced that it is your desire to understand your purpose and make the best out of the life that has brought you this far. I can assure you that you have made the right choice by picking up this book. Why? Because you are about to be introduced to quality information that will change your life forever!

So many people go through life disillusioned and confused. They cannot make any sense out of their lives because they seem so close but so far away from living a fulfilled and happy life. They have had moments when things seem to be going their way. They had moments here and there when they had the world at their feet and seemed to have arrived "there." They really wish such moments would continue forever, but it has never been like that.

They experience so many moments of disappointments and heartbreaks. They have invested in the wrong business, made wrong marital choices, and did the right things at the wrong times. The wrong choices ended up almost defining their lives. All the good times they have had have been totally consumed by the bad moments. If the story of your life so far has been like this, there is hope where you least expect. This book is definitely for you.

You are about to join the league of millions of people across the globe living a happy and fulfilled life because of their knowledge of numerology. Just imagine how your life will be if you had a good knowledge of what to do when to do it, and how to do it. You will definitely make fewer wrong choices in your career and relationships with others. You will know the kind of people you should be with that will help you and those who are not beneficial to you.

Once you make more right choices in your life, you will have more good times and less bad times. You will invest in the right deals and make more profit. You will be able to take advantage of relating with the right people and all the dividends that come with it. You will no longer go through life, confused. You will be more in charge of your life. You will no longer be a victim of circumstances. You will walk a clearly defined path in life that leads to a clearly specified destination. It will boost your confidence, and your self-esteem will skyrocket.

As the saying goes, "Luck only favors the brave." Hence, the knowledge you will gain from this book is not to make you lazy. Knowing your "lucky numbers" and other amazing things you will learn from this book is intended to help you "labor in the right direction." Life is beautiful and enjoyable when you have a fair idea of what works and does not work for you.

This book offers you the necessary insight you need as regards numerology as a beginner. The essence of writing this book is not to add to your knowledge about esoteric jargon, but to improve your experience as a person. Hence, if you have a reasonable level of education as regards the subject matter of numerology, you are also welcome. I guarantee that this book will also add value both to your knowledge and your life as a whole.

This book is a step-by-step guide to numerology. Hence, no stone will be left unturned to ensure that you have complete satisfaction by the time you have finished reading the book. The information in this book is presented in a simple manner to aid your understanding. For beginners, it is important to note that numerology is not the same as number theory, which is a branch of pure mathematics. Hence, I don't want you to have the notion that this book is an "advanced study of mathematics." As much as there is a strong link between numerology and mathematics, numerology is not a branch of mathematics.

As earlier stated, this book is written to add value to your life. Hence, I urge you to treat this book as a sort of "gold mine," where you will dig out "treasures." These treasures are very vital information that will improve your life. Therefore, you should never treat this book as one of those books you read to while away time. You should not read this book just because you can't find any other meaningful thing to do with your life. You should read this book with the intention of getting the knowledge that will radically change your life positively. The study of this book is a journey that will initiate a new cycle of stupendous positive moments in your life. You will not only begin to have palatable experiences, but you will have them consistently. I am excited to have the privilege to be your guide on this great journey into the world of the mystery of numbers. The best part of your life is about to begin.

Are you ready?!

Chapter 1: The History of Numerology

The study of numbers and how they affect one's life has a long history. However, it was not until 1907 before there was a mention of the word "numerology" in any English dictionary. The usage of numbers to obtain critical answers regarding the purpose of a person in various cultures fascinated mathematicians. Hence, they began to investigate the veracity of these claims of finding solutions to human problems with names and numbers.

The Early Days

Pythagoras is often seen as the "father" of numerology because of his huge contributions to numerology. He was born in Greece around 596 B.C. There are few historical records about him because most people that wrote about him did so years after his death. However, few of his works survived, and his contribution to numerology is one of such outstanding works.

Between (A.D. 354-430), Pythagoras, as well as some scientists of his time, were of the opinion that mathematical concepts have greater practicability. One such philosopher was Saint Augustine of Hippo. According to him, the Universal language with which the deity confirms the truth for humans is numbers.

Just like Pythagoras, he believed that every event in life has deep numerical connections. Hence, the human mind has the task of understanding the mystery of these connections. Otherwise, the source of this understanding will come by divine revelation. The mystical connections between numbers and the events in the life of people made numerology gain wide acceptance across the globe.

Persecution by the State Church

However, the practice of numerology took a hit when the state church via the influence of the Roman Emperor, Constantine, banned the practice. After the First Council of Nicaea in 325 AD, belief in astrology became classified in the same category as magic and astrology. Hence, it became an offense to believe in numerology.

However, this threat from the church was not strong enough to wipe off the belief. Numerology still held sway as Dorotheus of Gaza did an in-depth analysis of "Jesus number." Jesus' number is 888, which is the natural number preceding 889 and after 887. Strong arguments have been made as regards what has a semblance of numerology in the bible. For instance, 7 and 3 are believed to have strong spiritual significance. The length of famine in the bible is often 7 years, and it took God 7 days to create the world. Jesus was crucified by 3 pm, and he inquired of God to avoid being crucified three times. The number 8 is often connected to change after seven years of drought. Hence, in spite of the ban imposed on numerology by the state church, it was impossible to make people stop believing in the supernatural significance of numbers.

Besides the Bible, there are also theories of alchemy that have their roots in numerology. An example of this is how that Jabir Ibn Hayyan, a Persian-Arab alchemist, conducted various researches based on numerology ideologies in Arabic Language using the names of substances. In 1658, numerology was prominent in the "The Garden of Cyrus," a literary discourse by Sir Thomas Browne. The author of the book was bent on showing that the number 5 and the quincunx pattern is present in the design, arts, and in botany in particular.

Other Contributions

Various people contributed immensely to give numerology the modern outlook it has today. In "Numerology, the Power in Numbers," the author, Ruth A. Drayer, says that Mrs. L. Balliett combined Biblical references with the work of Pythagoras. Other valuable contributions came from Juno Jordan, a student of Balliett, who gave numerology the Pythagorean system. This system was not developed by Pythagoras but by Juno Jordan in 1965 via the publication of "Romance in Your Name."

The book contained the modern system of identifying the vital influence of numerology in birth dates and names. Other numerologists such as Kathleen Roquemore, Dusty Bunker, Faith Javane, Mark Gruner, Lynn Buess, and Florence Campbell have all done their part to make the evaluation of events and personality with numerology possible.

The Various Forms of Numerology

Various forms of numerology have been studied and practiced over the years. Different cultures and dispensations have had their own form of numerology, which was prevalent during that period and in that culture. The Babylonians, Chinese, Japanese, Indians, Egyptians, and the Jews all have a form of numerology they practice.

However, the three major forms of numerology are Kabbalic, Chaldean, and the Pythagorean. Each of these forms of numerology has its peculiarities. Each one has a unique way of number analysis and interpretations. However, the common feature of every system is to help people gain insight into their purpose in life and events around them.

The Kabbalic Form

The Kabbalic form is based on the Kabbalah, the Hebrew alphabets. Hence, this form of numerology is rooted in Jewish traditions. "Kabbalah" literally means "internal and spiritual knowledge." This implies that the knowledge is not derived from the senses but from your soul. In this system, every alphabet and number are believed to have a secret meaning that has practical application. The Kabbalic system deals with the birth name of a person in which 400 numbers and 22 alphabets are analyzed.

These numbers and alphabets are used to interpret the significance of that name and date of birth to the events that take place in that person's life. Each letter has a value that has a peculiar characteristic that explains certain aspects of a person's life. The Kabbalah form of numerology is the most difficult to interpret, but it offers great insight into the life of the person in question.

The end product of the Kabbalah system is to help you understand the talents you have. Hence, you will be able to put them to use and live a happy and fulfilled life. This form of numerology helps you understand your luck, makeup, and affection. Therefore, you will be able to identify areas of your life where you need to improve and be that man or woman you desire.

The Chaldean Form

The Chaldean form of numerology has its roots in ancient Babylon. It is the oldest of the three forms of numerology.

The Chaldean system is often referred to as "mystical numerology." This form of numerology is named after those who initiated its practice. Just around the 10th century BC, the Chaldean tribe inhabited ancient Babylon. This form of numerology is often considered as the most difficult to learn of all the forms of numerology.

The Chaldeans are famous for their mythologies and prophetic capabilities. The reason it is considered tough to master is that its investigation is in-depth as it begins from a person's date of birth. This form of numerology is the favorite of people who are in love with ancient knowledge. The Chaldean system, unlike the Kabbalah makes use of 8 numbers – 1-8. Besides, it only deals with the name the person is commonly called rather than the birth name.

This form of numerology is not common, but it is known for its predictive accuracy and precision. It is based on the vibrations produced by specific numbers with their peculiar features. The outer influences in the life of a person are depicted by the single digits, while the inner influences are depicted by the inner digits. The Chaldean system tells you about your personality and your ideal profession due to your capabilities and personality.

The Pythagorean Form

The Pythagorean system was developed by Pythagoras, a Greek mathematician, and philosopher. It is the most common of all forms of numerology. It is also known as "Western Numerology." Unlike the Kabbalic and Chaldean system, the Pythagorean system is easier to master, which explains why it is the most popular of the three. The reason the Pythagorean system is easy to master is that it employs the system of the Western alphabets and numbers.

Pythagoras believed that these numbers carry sacred energies that are incredibly powerful.

Concepts such as the Life Path Number, Destiny Number, and Soul Urge Number are predominant in this form of numerology. These numbers are used to make predictions about events that will occur in the life of a person. The formulas are quite easy to recall as they go with the numbers 1-9. The Pythagorean system uses a person's full name such that the alphabets of the name are converted to numbers. The numbers obtained from this conversion are used to get a destiny number, which is used to interpret the purpose of the person's life.

The Criticisms of Numerology

Those who are not convinced about the acclaimed power of numbers to provide answers to human problems have various sticks they try to use to beat numerology. Some argue that there is nothing spiritual about numbers; therefore, they have no ability to influence the incidents in a person's life. As long as such people are concerned, numerology is a mere superstition for people who are not ready to embrace scientific methods.

Those with the pseudoscience criticism will point to studies such as the ones that were carried out in Israel in 2012 and the United Kingdom in 1993. In the experiment that was carried out in the United Kingdom, 96 participants were involved. The aim of the experiment was to find out if there is a relationship between self-reported psychic ability and the number 7. At the end of the experiment, the researcher discovered that such a connection was false.

In the research that was carried out in Israel, 200 participants participated in the experiment. The objective of the experiment was to investigate the numerological accuracy of the diagnosis of learning disorders such as autism, ADHD, and dyslexia. At the end of the experiment, the diagnosis was found to be inaccurate. The researcher repeated the experiment twice to prove a point, but it was still the same.

Hence, skeptics will readily point out to such experiments to prove that numerology is nothing but a farce. However, as much as science has made life better by providing answers to numerous human problems, it is evident that science cannot explain everything. Science understands human physiology to a great deal, but science cannot provide sufficient explanation for death. Science has no explanation for emotions apart from pointing out the activities of hormones.

Hence, numbers and their significance is one of such things that science currently cannot explain. Numerology has played significant roles in history though critics would dismiss it as pseudoscience. Some scientists use "numerology" as a derogatory term for science they believe does not follow due to scientific procedure. For example, the coincidental similitude of some large numbers, which fascinated great scientists like Arthur Stanley Eddington, Herman Weyl, and Paul Dirac, was termed "numerology."

Such coincidences include the ratio of the age of the universe to the atomic unit of time, the difference between the strengths of gravity and the electric force of proton and electron, and the number of electrons in the universe. Funny enough, what became the popular periodic table today was as a result of what such scientists refer to as "numerology." The periodic table was formed through the categorization of elements by their physical properties after the discovery of the atomic triads.

In spite of the pessimism of some people, the veracity of numerology cannot be swept aside. I mean, you know that some certain numbers keep popping up in your life and they are affecting the outcome of situations in your life. A skeptic will dismiss it as mere coincidence. However, you know deep down in your heart that there is more to these numbers than they appear. I am sure that was what piqued your interest in reading this book in the first place. In the next chapter, we will extensively discuss the various methods of practicing numerology. The history class is over; let's proceed.

Chapter 2: Methods

In the previous chapter on the history of numerology, I touched the three major forms of numerology. However, just like I mentioned earlier, there are multiple methods of practicing numerology, with each method having its own peculiarities. In this chapter, I will intimate you on the Alphabetic systems, Pythagorean, Chaldean, Abjad, and mahadasha systems of numerology. I will conclude the chapter by comparing Chinese and Western numerology, and the connection numerology has to Astrology and Tarot.

Skeptics may say that the fact that there are different methods of practicing numerology shows that it is a false practice. However, researchers have various methods of investigating different research topics too. The experimental and correlation methods of research are used by scientists depending on the sensitivity and peculiarity of the research topic. Self-report methods and observational methods are also used to investigate various research topics.

Does the fact that scientists investigate various research topics with different methodologies make scientific claims invalid? The answer is obvious. Hence, the various methods of practicing numerology have their own peculiarities and practicability. However, every method is to the end that you will be able to gain further insight into your personality and talents. Numerology, in spite of its varying methodologies, has the unified aim of making your life more worthwhile.

Alphabetic Systems

The alphabetic system of practicing numerology exists in different cultures. The Arabs have the Abjad numerals; the Hebrews, Armenians, and Greeks all have their own alphabetic system too. Before the adoption of the popular Latin Alphabets, the German Runes were also popular. The main theme of every alphabetic system is that a numerical value is attached to an alphabet. Most times, this system only requires the birth name and birth date of the person.

From the birth name and date, 3 to 10 numbers will be extracted. The numerologist will examine the birth name and the likely present negative influences of that name on the life of the person. In case the numerologist discovers negative influences in your life as a result of your birth name, he or she will suggest how you can minimize or eradicate these influences.

For example, you may be told to tweak your name cards or your email signatures. If changing your name legally will not be a problem, it can be suggested to you to change the name so as to improve your experiences in life. The numbers extracted from your birth name and date can also be used to discover your personality traits and talents. Both your overt and covert traits can be unveiled by the numbers extracted from your birth date and name.

The essence of these discoveries is to help you channel your personality traits to the career path that will guarantee your success. Your desires and passion will be unveiled, and you will be able to know your purpose in life. It is also fascinating to know that these numbers can also be used to predict what lies in store for you in the future. The opportunities and potential pitfalls will be highlighted for you so that you can have a fair knowledge of your options and the best decisions for you.

A typical alphabetic system numerologist will give you an opportunity to make further inquiries at the end of the session. This will aid the numerologist to help you resolve any challenge you have as regards the assessment or other aspects of your life.

Abjad System

The Abjad system is the Arabic system of numerology. It is based on Abjad numerals or Abjad notations. In this system, each Arabic letter has a numerical value attached to it. This system is the foundation upon which "ilm-ul-huroof," the Science of Alphabet, and "ilm-ul-cipher," the Science of Cipher are built. The Abjad system has a numerical attachment to the alphabets as follows:

1=ط=9 ح=8 ز=7 و=6 ه=5 د=4 ج=3 ب=2 أ

10=ص=90 ف=80 ع=70 س=60 ن=50 م=40 ل=30 ك=20 ي

ظ=900 ض=800 ذ=700 خ=600 ث=500 ت=400 ش=300
100=ر =200 ق

غ=1000

If you observe carefully, the alphabets are 28 in all. Each of these alphabets has a numerical value attached to it. This system of numerology has been in existence before the eight century. Abjad was actually derived from the first four letters of the Semitic Alphabet (A, B, J, D). These letters are also the first four in the Hebrew, Aramaic, and Phoenician alphabets.

The Abjad system is an alphabetic system. Hence, the essence of the numbers attached to the alphabets is to have a deeper understanding of an individual. The value of the numbers attached to your name has significance in this system. These numbers reveal your behavioral inclinations. They reveal your innermost desire and what your "calling" is in life.

From the assessment of the Abjad numerologists, you will be able to know more about yourself and the best professional path that suits you the most. You will be able to know the kind of business you can invest in and the kind of people that can complement you. You will have further insight as regards your strengths and your weaknesses. You will also be able to know what to expect in your life in the future. Hence, you will be able to prepare for any changes, whether positive or negative. You will have a clear direction in life.

Pythagorean System

The Pythagorean system of numerology is also called "Pythagorean numerology or Western numerology." This system of numerology was developed by Pythagoras, a Greek scientist. Pythagoras noticed that there is a connection between musical notes and numbers. He realized that the peculiar vibrations produced by stringed instruments have mathematical explanations.

The Pythagorean system of numerology depends on your birth name and birth date to reveal important information about you. This system attempts to explain your outer nature. Your outer nature is the personality traits everyone can see you exhibit. These personality traits are obtained from the numbers attached to your name.

This system of numerology works by first obtaining your name the exact way you have it on your birth certificate.

Each letter of your birth name will have a number attached to it based on the ancient Pythagorean system from number one to nine. This system makes use of Latin alphabets such that the number 1 is attached to the letters a, j, and s. The number 2 is attached to the letters b, k, and t. Number 3 is assigned to the letters c, l, u; number 4 to d, m, and v; number 5 to e, n, and w; 6 to f, o, and x; 7 to g, p, y; 8 to h, q, z; and number 9 to letter I and r.

The numbers that are attached to your full name as seen in your birth certificate will be added together systematically to obtain a name number. For example, if your name on your birth certificate is Anthony Martial Lionel, your name number will be obtained as follows:

Anthony = 1 + 5 + 2 + 8 + 6 + 5 + 7 = 34

Martial = 4 + 1 + 9 + 2 + 9 + 1 + 3 = 29

Lionel = 3 + 9 + 6 + 5 + 5 + 3 = 31

Anthony Martial Lionel = 34 + 29 + 31 = 94

Name number = 9 + 4 = 13 = 1 + 3 = 4

From the above calculations, the name number for an individual whose name is Anthony Martial Lionel is 5. If Anthony Martial Lionel decides to alter some part of his name, this will lead to a new number name. The initial number name is used to explain part of his life. Hence, an alteration will lead to alteration is some aspects of the individual's life.

In the Pythagorean system, your birth date is seen as an extension of your personality. Hence, it is also calculated to obtain a single digit. The number obtained from your birth date is used to unveil the talents or personality traits you wish you possess. This number shows the personality traits you possess but does not exhibit to the world.

It also reveals your purpose in life. It is important to note that in this system, there are numbers that are referred to as "master numbers." They are the numbers 11, 22, and 33. If, after calculating your birth number, it ended up being any of these three numbers, it will not be reduced to a single digit. The inferences about your life will be drawn from these numbers.

Chaldean System

The Chaldean system of numerology is also called the Babylonian numerology system. This is because it originated from the Chaldeans, who inhabited Babylonia from 625 to 539 BC. This system is used to identify the various changes in energy that takes place when you are speaking or when another person is talking. The frequency of the vibration that occurs when people speak around you varies and affects you and those close to you.

The Chaldeans use numbers 1 to 8. They don't use the number 9 because they believe that the number is connected to infinity. This system does not employ the use of birth name but the current name of the person. They do this because they believe that the vibrations that will be generated around the person are based on the current name of the person. Just like the Pythagorean system of numerology, the Chaldean system also attaches numbers to Latin alphabets.

However, because they only use the numbers 1-8, the numbers that are attached to the letters are not the same as that of the Pythagorean system. In the Chaldean system, the number 1 is assigned to the letters a, q, I, y, j. Number 2 is attached to the letters b, r, and k; 3 is attached to g, c, l, s; 4 is attached to d, m, t; 5 is assigned to e, h, n, x; 6 is attached to u, v, w; 7 is assigned to o and z; and 8 is attached to the letters f and p.

Hence, in the example of Anthony Martial Lionel, the name number that will be derived in the Chaldean system will be different from the one that will be derived from the Pythagorean system. However, this does not mean that the answer you will get from a Pythagorean numerologist will be significantly different from what is obtainable with a Chaldean numerologist.

Just like the Pythagorean system, the master numbers 11, 22, and 33 are also recognized and not altered. In other words, just like the Pythagorean system, if your birth name is 11, 22, or 33, it will not be reduced to a single digit. In this system, your first name shows the personality you present to the public. It also reveals your habits and personal interests.

Your Soul energy is revealed by the vowels in your name. This name is very vital because it reveals your innermost desires and talents. Your purpose in life is found here because the things your soul craves for is located here. The influence of your domestic family on your life is unveiled by your last name.

Mahadasha System

The Mahadasha system is a communication of numerology and astrology. "Dasha" refers to a state or planetary period. The Dasha pattern reflects the particular planets that will rule at specific periods based on the Jyotish. Jyotish is the Hindu system of astrology, which is also called Vedic astrology. Mahadasha is vital in the prediction of future events via the use of a natal chart in this type of astrology.

Mahadasha can create doshas or yogas that can change effects on transit planets. Anyone who wants to be wealthy, popular, or successful must have the support of mahadasha to make it possible. There are 9 types of mahadasha: Rahu Mahadasha, Chandra Mahadasha, Guru Mahadasha, Budha Mahadasha, Sani Mahadasha, Ketu Mahadasha, Sukra Mahadasha, Surya Mahadasha, and Kuja Mahadasha.

The grand total of all Mahadashas is 120 years life span. Mahadashas like Ketu, Sun, Moon, and Mars are less than ten years. However, Mahadashas, like Rahu, Saturn, Jupiter, Mercury, and Venus, are more than fifteen years. The effect each Mahadasha is determined by looking at the dasha lord, its Karaka, and its respective depositor as seen in the yoga-formation of the planet. The placement of Venus, for example, is important for the Venus Mahadasha.

A good or bad result is derived from the yoga formation during the mahadasha of the planets involved in the yoga-formation. The sign the Moon occupies is vital for the prediction of future events in this system. If the Moon is devoid of strength, every other planet is considered weak.

Chinese vs. Western Numerology

Chinese numerology is not based on just the numbers but rather the sounds they make when said out loud. Hence, if a number sounds like a word that is negative when said aloud, that number is seen as a sign of something negative. However, when the sound of the number has a semblance with a positive word when said aloud, it is associated with something positive. Therefore, luck is a key component of Chinese numerology.

The importance of luck is one of the major differences between Chinese and Western numerology. Western numerology is based on the Pythagorean system of numerology. In Western numerology, luck does not play a significant role. Each number has both positive and negative attributes in Western numerology. Therefore, in Western numerology is up to you to exhibit either the positive or negative attributes of the number associated with your name.

For example, in Chinese numerology, the number "1" has a semblance with the Chinese word for "honor." Hence, the number is associated with loneliness or independence. The number is associated with the water element; hence, it represents the ability to succeed in spite of the barriers in your way. In Western numerology, number 1 has a different meaning. The number represents creation or new beginning in Western numerology.

The positive attributes of number 1 in Western numerology include leadership, courage, and initiative. Meanwhile, negative attributes include impulsiveness and confrontational behavior. Therefore, while the Chinese numerology attributes the events in the life of a person to factors somewhat outside of the control of the person, Western numerology puts the individual in the driving seat of his or her life. Western numerology is very popular in the West, while Chinese numerology is popular in the east.

Numerology & Its Connection to Astrology & Tarot

Those learning Astrology & Tarot for the first time may find it daunting. However, it becomes easier when you understand the connection between numerology and the tarot. The deck of the tarot is divided into the minor and the major categories. Each of these categories is called "Arcana." The tarot deck consists of 78 cards. The understanding of the difference between each Arcana and their number will help you understand any card.

The minor Arcana deals with the physical realm, which divided into four suit cards, which contain the Wands, Cups, Pentacles, and Swords. The Wands represent will, the Cups represent emotion, the Pentacles represent material, and the Swords represent intellect. The minor Arcana has a semblance of the deck of regular playing cards but differs in that it has a Page, which is an additional court card. Every suit has a numbering of 1 to 10 and a corresponding element.

The Major Arcana are cards with large pictures, which represents vital moments in the life of a person. These cards are crucial and carry deep meanings when interpreted. There are 22 cards in the Major Arcana with the numbering of 0 to 21. The symbols on the cards of the Major Arcana represent the story of the transition from one phase of life to the other. It all begins at childhood and innocence and ends at maturation and enlightenment.

The numerological underpinning of the tarot lies in the numbering of the cards in the major and minor Arcana. The numbers on each of the cards of the minor and major Arcana have specific meanings, which is the core idea of numerology. There are five cards corresponding to the number 1: The Ace of Cups, Swords, Wands, Pentacles, and the Magician Card. The Magician cards are in the Major Arcana while the rest are in the minor Arcana.

The meaning of each of the four Aces is not the same, but they ultimately have the same message: new beginnings. Another approach to the interpretation of the tarot is to treat it as a cycle. The odd numbers generally represent instability and change, while the even numbers generally represent stability and endurance. The cyclical nature of the tarot is such that every ending depicts a new beginning.

Numerology in a Tarot Interpretation

In the tarot, the number 1 represents new beginnings as well as the first step on your journey. The minor Arcana Aces are the purest form of the element of every suit. They commonly appear when you are starting a relationship, a new job, or a desire to approach something with a new perspective. Generally, it is all about going in a direction that is not the same as the one you were going before.

The number 2 is the number of partnerships and the decisions you make on your path in life. It is during the process of consideration that number two shows up. This number demands the direction you want to take from you as well as the people joining your team. The number 3 is the number of growth. It can be the growth of a relationship, project, or idea. The number depicts natural progression and team building.

The number 4 represents foundations. This card depicts practicability and logical reasoning as a result of stability. The early burst of energy with which you started something important is now stable. This number shows up when you have achieved a level of success. The number 5 represents instability and change. This number depicts the struggles and conflicts that arise as a result of a clash of personality and perspective. It also shows up when an unforeseen challenge enters your path.

The number six is the number of relieve after a turbulent period. This card depicts that friends and family will come around to help out, and you will experience stability again. This card shows the importance of the support of the people around you to your success in life. Number 7 is the number of faith and patience. It signifies patience as you wait for your efforts to bring you the success you desire. It shows that patience and faith during the waiting phase are all part of creation.

The number 8 depicts progress and imminent success. The hard work you have put in during the previous phase of the previous numbers is about to pay off. There is excitement in this phase because you are close to completing the cycle you began from one. The number 9 is the number of completion. It shows that you have come to the end of a cycle. Your decisions and efforts will yield positive and negative results in this phase. The number 10 is the end of a cycle before a new one begins.

Chapter 3: The Meaning of Numbers In Numerology and How Numbers Work

Numbers are the "fuel" on which the numerology vehicle runs. Hence, it is impossible to understand numerology without a sound understanding of how numbers work in numerology. There is no number that is irrelevant in numerology. Although the meaning assigned to every number differs from one system of numerology to the other, ultimately, every number has its place and significance and has esoteric powers.

In this chapter, I will take you through an in-depth analysis of the workings of numbers in numerology. I will take you through concepts such as master numbers, double-digit numbers, and Karmic numbers. You will also learn about Palindromes and get explanations for why you keep seeing the same numbers.

General Guidelines

I will start with the single-digit numbers and their characteristics before I explain other combinations like thee double-digit numbers and master numbers. The foundation of numerology is built on single-digit numbers. The single-digit numbers begin at 1 and end in 9.

Generally, 1 is a leadership number. It is the number of creation from a spiritual perspective. It is focused on setting goals and not easily distracted. It has a knack for grinding out results. However, it is often unforgiving, impatient, demanding, and a jealous lover. 2 is the most cooperative of the 9 single-digit numbers. It is gentle, forgiving, and gentle. It is resilient and non-confrontational. However, it can be mean, jealous, and vengeful when others covet what belongs to it or mistreat it.

3 is creative and extraordinarily talented. A career in art is the best destination for such people. It has wit and excellent social skills. However, it is superficial and always wants to be the center of attraction. 4 is stable and strong. It is dependable, patient, and conventional. It finds satisfaction in personal progress rather than public recognition. They thrive in organized settings like the military but struggles in social settings.

5 is the most vibrant and freedom-loving of the single-digit numbers. It is always seeking change and relentless. It is daring and never submissive. It will never cheat on a partner like 2 and 6 no matter the temptation but can break a relationship easily because of the strong will. It felt free to date anyone when not in a relationship and annoyed if told to limit going out on a date.

6 is loving and caring, which is the reason it is called "the fatherhood/motherhood number." It is protective, sacrificial, and patient to teach. However, it is myopic and focuses on the smaller picture while ignoring the bigger picture. 7 is philosophical as it likes to seek and search the truth. It does not take anything at face value and places a premium on critical thinking. However, it is not honest and often opinionated.

8 puts emphasis on career, business, and power. It is a karmic equalizer that easily creates and destroys. It is generous and willing to take risks. However, it can be intolerant, aggressive, and greedy. 9 is special from a

mathematical point of view. This is because if you multiply any number by nine, the addition of the result of the multiplication will give you 9.

For example, if you multiply 9 by 5, you will get 45. 4 plus five gives you nine. You can try it with other numbers. From a numerology point of view, 9 has global consciousness; it sees no difference between its neighbor and someone living in a different culture. It is the most tolerant and least judgmental of all the nine single-digits. However, 9 can be apathetic, arrogant, and cold. It can also be egoistic and immoral.

Double-Digit Numbers

Every single digit has its own peculiar characteristics and personality traits. However, sometimes, a single-digit number can be as a result of the combination of double-digit numbers. Such combinations often alter the personality traits of the single-digit number a little bit. For example, number 7 can be based on 70, 61, 52, 43, 34, 25, or 16.

However, their situations in which the change can be very dramatic in the case of a Master number or a Karmic debt number. It is always good to include a single-digit number that is based on a double-digit number in the numerology chart. For example, if a 7 is based on 52, it should be written as 52/7 and 43/7 if it is based on 43. The characteristics of a double-digit number are based on that of a single-digit number.

The double-digit number will retain some of the characteristics of the single-digit number and diminish some of its characteristics. However, it never totally eliminates the properties of the single-digit number. For instance, a 7 based on 34 is more creative than any other 7, while a 7 based on 16 is more withdrawn than a 7 based on 25. Numbers that can be divided by 10 without the remainder, such as 20 and 70, strengthen the characteristics. For example, a 50 is a high octave 5, and a 60 is a high octave 6.

Double-digit 10 is a high octave 1; it enhances the characteristics of number 1. This implies that the person will be a powerful leader with a sharp focus that inspires success. Such people can be ruthless in achieving their goals and have the tendency to become tyrants. Number 12 is highly creative, unconventional, and individualistic. They often have poor time management skills and poor team members.

People with a double-digit number 24 comfort and are adept in comforting and counseling others. They often like to play musical instruments with a particulate interest in percussion. They are often unstable in relationships and can be a bit gossipy. They will not be able to thrive in the absence of a solid, stable environment. Number 25 excels in spiritual leadership. It is the most cooperative of all the 7s but can be self-indulgent and too serious. They often find it difficult to share feelings and have a restless streak.

Double-digit 28 is a 10 but more tolerant and compassionate. It is a warrior number that is more determined and ambitious than the other 10s. 30 is a high octave 3 endowed with communication skills and creativity. It is a bit superficial but warm and possesses a good sense of humor. However, it can be easily distracted and lacks resilience and consistency.

31 is more fun-loving and extrovert than the other 4s. They are also more creative than other fours, but they often have issues in relationships. A key reason for their relationship issues is their lack of faithfulness. They cannot be trusted to stay committed to friends and partners in the long haul.

Master Numbers

All numbers carry significant meaning in numerology. However, experts in numerology believe that some numbers are more special than others. These numbers are referred to as **Master numbers.** In numerology, there are three master numbers – 11, 22, and 33. These numbers are not just powerful; they have added potential because they are combinations of two numbers.

People who have master numbers in their date of birth or name are gifted and possess special attributes that make them different from other people. Such people are unusually intelligent and possess heightened intuition. Each of the master numbers has its own significance and attributes accompanying it.

Master number 11 is the most intuitive among the master numbers. This number is often referred to as **The Old Soul** master number. People with this master number have an unusual connection with their subconscious and gut feeling. They possess rare insight and have the capacity to deal with sensitive situations with unusual calmness. They are usually relaxed in their approach to stressful situations, which makes others depend on them for inspiration.

People with this master number are prophets, clairvoyants, and psychics. Empathy and respect are strong attributes people with this master number possess in abundance. The negative attribute of this master number is that such people are in danger of experiencing fear and anxiety if they are not able to concentrate their efforts on a particular task. Popular people with this master number include Michael Jordan, Chetan Kumar, Edgar Allan Poe, Madonna, Orlando Boom, and Gwen Stefani.

Master number 22 is also called **The Master Builder**. People who possess this master number have an unusual ability to achieve set goals. They possess the heightened intuition of people with master number 111, but they are more disciplined and practical. Such people often have big plans, huge potentials, and great ideas. They have high self-esteem and leadership skills, which are the requisite ingredients for success. This master number associated with great thinkers who were able to fulfill their potential.

Such people know how to go about making their dreams come to fruition. They are often early bloomers with outstanding results. The negative trait of people with this master number is that some of them lack the practical ability to fulfill their undoubtedly huge potential. Popular people with this master number include John Kerry, Hu Jintao, Leonardo Da Vinci, and Will Smith.

Master number 33 is also called "The Master Teacher." People with this number are rare, as the number is the most influential and powerful. The reason for the immense power and influence of this master number is that it also contains the master numbers 11 and 22. Hence, anyone who has the master number 33 is an upgrade on the two aforementioned master numbers.

People with master number 33 do not have any ambition of their own; their ambition is to cause a spiritual uplifting of all mankind. Such people display total devotion and unusual insight and understanding without communication. They are more concerned about humanitarian projects and will give themselves totally to it.

Such people are tremendously knowledgeable in a very unusual way. However, they can be very emotional and tends to have bursts of anger. Popular people who possess this master number include Thomas Edison, John Lennon, Albert Einstein, Robert De Niro, Francis Ford Coppola, Salma Hayek, and Stephen King.

Karmic Debt Numbers

In numerology, you are perceived as a spiritual being that incarnates on the earth for the purpose of moving toward a higher state of enlightenment and awareness. Your long evolutionary journey has afforded you loads of wisdom such that you have made many right choices that have future benefits. In the same vein, you have also made wrong choices such that you will have to take on an additional burden to make up for the lessons you did not learn in your previous lives. This burden is what is known as a **Karmic Debt** in numerology.

The numbers that show you have a Karmic Debt include 13, 14, 16, and 19. The importance of these double-digit numbers when finding in your Life Path, Personality, or birthday is massive. Each of these Karmic Debt numbers has its own peculiar challenges and characteristics. For example, those with Karmic Debt number 13 will strive hard to accomplish any task. They usually have obstacles that stand in their way, which they have to overcome repeatedly. Such a person will find frustration in a commonplace and will be tempted to give up due to the almost impossible nature of the task to be accomplished.

Such people are often found to be lazy and pessimistic about life, but success for them is not actually impossible. They just have to work hard and be focused on achieving success in the task that comes their way. The reason some people with the Karmic Debt number 13 fail in life is that they are not able to focus on a specific goal. They focus their energy and resources on various projects such that they end up not succeeding in any. Such people will be tempted to take shortcuts, but they often have their fingers burned and can resort to self-pity.

Karmic Debt number 14 is a product of abuse of human freedom in previous lives. Hence, such people have no choice but to adapt to unstable circumstances and unforeseen events. They are in real danger of becoming drug addicts and the inability to control oneself when tempted with sex or food. People with this Karmic Debt number have to be courteous and modest to avoid going down the drain in life. Orderliness and emotional stability are also crucial to maintain focus during those periods of change for such people.

Karmic Debt number 16 points to the elimination of the old and the birth of the new. This Karmic Debt number is like a cleansing to remove every all that has been constructed to severe the person from the source of life. Such people have personal struggles with their ego and divine will. The grand plan of people with this Karmic Debt number crumbles such that they eventually learn to be humble to achieve true success in the long run. A spiritual rebirth takes place during this ruin, and the new person is born. Such people often look down on others because of their refined intellect, but that will lead to paying a high price to make them humble.

Karmic Debt number 19 points to the learning of proper use of power and independence. People with this Karmic Debt number will be forced to stand for what they believe alone. They will face difficulties but will overcome through grit and determination. Such people tend to reject the advances of others to help them because of their tendency to put themselves in a self-imposed prison. They find it difficult to come to terms with the need for mutual love and interdependence. They will end up learning the hard way that they can't succeed in life all alone.

Repeating Numbers

Repeating numbers like 111, 222, 333, 444, or 555 have interesting meanings in numerology. Each repeating number has its own particular characteristic and meaning. For example, 111 is a wakeup call from the universe. When you take note of this number, do a proper evaluation of your life and your approach to things. This number is positive because it shows that you are on the right path in life. It is a way of the universe, encouraging you to go on because success is within your reach. However, you need to be careful of overconfidence because being on the right path does not mean that you have reached your destination already.

111 also implies that you have the capacity to bring meaning and happiness to people around you. You have the gift of inspiring others and helping them achieve their dreams in life. Therefore, when you see this number appearing in your life, stay conversant with the way you are

going about life and continue on that path. However, be also deliberate about helping others find the right path in life as you go on your journey.

2 is the number of relationships and partnerships. Hence, 222 is a clarion call to be observant about the kind of people you are allowing influencing you. It is a wakeup call from the universe telling you that your soul mate is nearby if you don't have one already. It means you should place a premium on valuing the people around you and reconnecting with your old friends. It can also mean you need to open up more to have new friends who will be beneficial to you. If you are in a relationship already when you start seeing this sequence of numbers, it means you have to be careful because the relationship is important, and you hold on to it.

333 is a trinity number that is pointing you to align your mind, body, and soul together. It is the universe telling you that an aspect of your life needs attention too, and fix. It may be that you have been too busy to pay attention to the needs of your loved ones lately. It may also mean that you are paying too much attention to a new relationship such that you are neglecting other important things in your life.

444 is a number meaning that you need to pay attention to people in your inner circle because "4" is the number of home and family. If you keep seeing this number, you need to consider spending quality time with your closest friends and family. It is a number also pointing you remember your roots. You may be missing out on some core lessons that made you who you are. It may also mean you need to change the atmosphere of your home to make it more positive.

555 is the universe pointing your attention to the fact that you have enough momentum to move in a new direction. It shows you should be looking out for new opportunities, and you should ensure you are well placed to capitalize on them. This number shows that you should not resist change because the right time to move in a new direction has come. In case you have been waiting to do something new, you are poised to do it when this number keeps popping up.

Palindromes

Palindromes are numbers, sentences, or words that read the same, whether forward or backward. They include numbers such as 11, 44, 77, 111, 131, 151, 161, 202 etc. You may find something like 6:26 26% on your computer screen or $47.74 as the price of a product you want to purchase. These numbers have psychic meanings. These numbers are angel numbers with which your angel uses to get your attention. If you are able to pay attention to these palindromes, the mission of the angel is accomplished. You should not treat these numbers lightly because they have significant spiritual meanings to your past, present, and future.

Your spirit guide, which is assigned to help you navigate life smoothly, uses palindromes to communicate to you. The answers you are seeking about the next direction in your life are often right around you. If only you pay more attention to details, you will live a more meaningful and fulfilled life. A palindrome like 777 is the universe telling you that you need to do more than reading books but practice what you have been learning. 999 indicates the completion of a particular cycle of events in your life.

I keep Seeing the Same Numbers - What Does it Mean?

The universe has an interesting way of communicating with us through numbers. You can find yourself seeing repeating numbers on pieces of paper, a billboard, or zip code. These repeating numbers are pointers that something divine is happening in your life. If you often find a sequence of repeating numbers in your life, you need to take note.

The number may be single-digits, double digits, or palindromes. Irrespective of the number or sequence, it is a sign of divine communication. Your spirit guide is trying to point your attention to something in your life. It may be a part of your life you are neglecting or a part of your life you are giving too much attention. Numerologists help interpret these numbers so that you can have a clear understanding of the message of the universe to you.

The earlier you pay attention to these numbers, the better for you. You will make fewer mistakes in your relationships, family, and career when you have a good grasp of the message of your spirit guide to you. The great things of life are in those simple numerical details and sequences. Fools dismiss these numbers as mere "coincidences," while wise people dig deeper to respond to the intense effort of the universe to reach out to them.

Interesting Numbers: 23, 44, 666

Numbers such as 23, 44, and 666 are interesting in numerology because of their peculiar significance. People who have 23 as their core number loves people and are committed to promoting a good cause. They often freedom fighters, and they are the most creative of the 5s. However, they have the tendency to be realistic and quit when the going gets tough.

44 is a power number. It is excellent for people who want to have a career in the military or own a business franchise. Such people are visionary and always see to it that they accomplish any goals they set for themselves. Such people see opportunities where others are struggling and have unusual resilience, especially when the going gets tough. They are not fazed by challenges and relish taking the risk. They can think quickly and have the foresight to build something that will last in the long run. They set realistic goals and are practical in their attempt to achieve those goals. They are not just dreamers; they are all out to achieve their dream.

In the Bible, 666 is the number of the Beast or the Devil. Hence, if you repeatedly see this number, you need to be wary because it means that something evil is around the corner. 666 is also the number of life and mankind. The basis of life is carbon, and it has 6 electrons, 6 protons, and 6 neutrons. Generally, 666 indicates that you should be careful about the moments presenting themselves to you around that time.

Chapter 4: Getting Started With Numerology / Discovering Your Personal Numerology Blueprint

The greatest thing that can happen to you in life is to discover yourself. A very vital way to discover yourself is to discover your personal numerology blueprint. The knowledge of the numbers in your life puts you in charge of your life. You will hardly be taken aback by events unfolding in your life. You will be able to envisage events and prepare for them adequately. In this chapter, I will be taking you through the properties of numbers. I will also help you through how you can create your numerology profile and destiny map reading.

The Properties of Numbers

A major reason why the knowledge of the supernatural power of numbers seems elusive is that more people only have knowledge based on conjectures. Most of the things some people know about numerology are mere assertions based on mythology and not facts. For example, when it comes to the properties of numbers in numerology, some wrongly allude that there are "good" and "bad numbers in numerology.

In other words, such people believe that there are numbers whose properties are positive while there are numbers whose attributes are negative. Some allude that the number "13" is an unlucky number. As a result of this belief, some would not let their buildings have the 13th floor, while some are very pessimistic about the 13th of every month. They believe something evil will happen on that day to them or their loved ones.

In the popular scenario of the "Lord's Supper," some will point to the fact that there were 13 participants in the famous supper. One of the 13 participants, Judas, was the one who betrayed Jesus. Hence, some see this as further proof that 13 is an unlucky number, which signifies that even is lurking around the corner. Is this assertion really true? Is 13 an unlucky number? The answer lies in the true understanding of the properties of numbers in numerology.

In numerology, 13 is a "4" because the addition of 1 and 4 will add up to 4. Ultimately, 13 is one of the Karmic Debt numbers. Just like other Karmic Debt numbers, it is a number that indicates that the individual will strive hard to accomplish any task. It shows that the person will have obstacles and find frustration in a commonplace and will be tempted to give up. The reason for this is that it will be as though it is impossible to succeed in the task they have to achieve.

People who have 13 in their core numbers can be pessimistic and carefree about life. However, such people can be successful and achieve their dreams in life if they are determined and work hard. They will be able to succeed if they focus on specific tasks instead of jumping from one project to the other. Hence, 13 is not an unlucky number. It all depends on the individual who has the number as part of his or her core number to strive hard to achieve success in spite of difficulties. I guess you are relieved if you are one of such people.

Contrary to popular opinion, it is not true that some numbers only possess positive attributes, while some possess only negative attributes. In numerology, every number apart from zero has its positive and negative properties. Zero is a state of nothingness; hence, it does not possess positive or negative attributes all by itself in numerology.

Any number that appears in your core numbers, such as destiny number or life path number, possesses both positive and negative attributes. There is nothing set in stone in numerology. In other words, the positive or negative properties of any number or sequence of numbers that appear in your core number will not take place in your life automatically. In other words, you are the one who decides whether you will experience the positive attributes of your core numbers or the negative attributes.

Hence, numerology is not a magical practice that assigns an unchangeable future to you. In fact, you need to find out the meaning of your core numbers so that you can modify and change the events surrounding your life. Through the change of name, for example, you can alter the experiences of your life because your name contains the "code" that determines your talent and personality traits.

How to Create a Numerology Profile and Fulfill your Future Plans

Numerology is such that you can become an expert on your own. You can interpret the meaning of the numbers in your life and also that of others around you. You don't even need to be a mathematical guru or obtain a degree in mathematics to know the meaning of the numbers in your life. All you need is a desire to learn and explore. Once your heart is set to learn and make changes in your life and that of others, you are good to go.

The important numbers in your life include your Life Path number, Destiny number, and Lucky number. However, the most important number in your numerology reading is your Life Path number. Your Life Path is the road you are traveling in life. It is the "route" that explains the unique opportunities and challenges that will come your way in life. Your Life Path says a lot about your personality and the best career path for you.

You can derive your Life Path number through the simple addition of the day, month, and year of your birth. The day you were born was the day you stepped into consciousness. You began a new life, and all that you need to become all that you should become is already part of your DNA. Hence, every opportunity and challenge of your life are embedded in your birth date. If you are familiar with Astrology, a Life Path number is more like Zodiac signs you will find in Stars Signs Book.

If your birth date is July 7, 1995, for example, your Life Path number will be 2. How? The month of July is the 7th month of the year; hence, it will be represented by number 7. Every number of the birth year will be added together with the day and month to obtain your life path number. You will first obtain a double-digit number, which has to be further reduced to obtain a single-digit number. The calculation goes thus:

7 +7 + (1 + 9 + 9 + 5)

= 14 + 24

= 38

38 has to be further reduced to obtain a single-digit number.

3 + 8

= 11

= 1 + 1

= 2

In a numerology chart, there are eleven numbers, which are 1, 2, 3, 4, 5, 6, 7, 8, 9, 11, and 22. Any number that is bigger than these numbers are added together and reduced to one of these numbers. When you live your life within the parameters of your Life Path number, you will feel energized and on track. However, when you are outside the parameters of your Life Path Number, you will be frustrated and unable to record any meaningful success.

Up next is your **expression Number.** This number is derived by the addition of the values assigned to your birth name. This number indicates your expressions in life and the best career path for you. Another number you need to pay attention to is your **motivation Number.** This number is also called your **soul urge number.** This number refers to the greatest desire of your soul. It points you in the direction of what you should become in life to attain fulfillment. Your soul urge number is derived by adding all the vowels in your full name together.

Your **Life Destiny number** refers to those things you need to accomplish to be fulfilled in life. It is derived from the addition of all the numbers in your full birth name. Your **Personal Lucky Number** refers to the number that will bring you luck in your entire life. This number is constant and does not change at any point in your life. You have to be careful because your personal lucky number does not indicate that something positive will happen whenever you see the number. It only implies that your chances of obtaining a positive result are high when you see this number. Your Personal Lucky Number is your Life Path Number.

Destiny Map Reading (More about You)

Every society has structures where they fit in every individual. These structures are meant to give both people who are present and those unborn an identity and a place in life. Unfortunately, many people are celebrated for their ability to fit into these structures perfectly. However, in fitting into these structures, many have lost their true identity. One of the worst things that can happen to a person is to do effectively well what he or she ought not to have done at all.

Many people achieve what many covet in life, but they feel so empty at the end of it all. They feel there is more they could have done and died in regret that they were never able to discover those things that were missing. The truth is that you don't have to wait until the end of your life before you discover your true identity. Thankfully, numerology offers you a "map" to your destiny. Numerology charts are the roadmaps where your uniqueness, identity, and weaknesses are unveiled.

Numerology charts offer you the tool to answer those difficult questions about your life. You have always known that there is more to your life than meets the eyes. You know that you are unique and have abilities waiting to be unlocked, but the knowledge seems elusive. An acquaintance with your core numbers brings an end to this almost endless search about who you are. Whatever seems hidden about your personality and the choices you need to make to turn your life around is closer than you imagine.

Numerology is all about knowing "you." You cannot claim to know you when you don't have a clue about the career path that is best for you or the kind of person that is best for you. Your knowledge of yourself is not complete when you don't know your strengths and weaknesses. Your numerology profile is complete when you know your Life Path Number, Soul Urge Number, and Expression number.

In other words, you have been empowered with all the weapons you need to go through life successfully. Checking through the numerology chart to understand the important numbers in your life is your ticket to your inner world. Once you know the path the universe has laid down for you to walk and your gifts, you are unstoppable. You will have clarity and know the exact direction you need to head in life.

Knowing the core numbers in your life may help you become a household name and reach unprecedented success. However, it is not always the case that you will attain fame and much wealth. However, one thing is certain; you will not end your life wishing you lived in different. The uncertainty and frustration that are commonplace in the life of many will be far from you. You will be convinced that you are living your life the way you are supposed to live it.

Fame and wealth are good, and we all desire to have them. However, happiness and fulfillment in life are more important than wealth and fame. What is the point of earning wealth and becoming famous, but you are not happy and fulfilled. There is no point living a life to make others happy and proud of you, but you feel empty. Hence, you should be happy with the fact that your knowledge of your destiny, strength, and weakness will give you an edge in life and live a happy and fulfilled life.

It is amazing to know that you don't have to pay a psychic or numerology expert to find out all you need to know about yourself. Numerology is such that any information you need is all around you as long as you search in the right direction.

Chapter 5: Your Birthday Number

One of the most important numbers in your life in numerology is your birthday number. Via your birthday number, so many important things in your life, such as your personality, career path, relationship choice, location, and business, can be revealed. Your birthday number is a code that says a lot about you. If you think the day you were born was a mere coincidence, you are wrong. People who were born with unfortunate events surrounding their birth often feel they are products of the mistakes of their parents.

However, every mistake is a blessing in disguise. You were not born mistakenly, even if it appears like that. The understanding of what our birthday number reveals about you will let you see how truly unique and special you are. Hence, in this chapter, I will help you to understand what your birthday number reveals about you and how that will help you appreciate your strengths and embrace your weaknesses.

Date of Birth Analysis

Your date of birth contains information about you that makes you different from other people. Your purpose in life is located right within the code of your date of birth. It is not out of place if you are one of those people in life seeking to understand the reason they are living. Life is all about expressing the reason for living. The intelligence for being is within that thing. All that a seed needs to grow into a mighty tree is within that seed. In the same way, all you need to become that woman or man you are meant to be is within you.

For everything in life, there is a purpose. Every change in season has its advantage and disadvantages. Many people don't like autumn because of the temperature, but that is the time for the harvest of many fruits and vegetables. The same way every inventor has something in mind for his or her invention; you are also on earth to fulfill a purpose. Thankfully, the universe has not hidden this crucial knowledge about our purpose in life from us.

What you need to change the direction of your life to live a happy and fulfilled life is located in understanding that you are. Your date of birth was the day you began to live as you took your first breath. Your date of birth carries the information about your purpose for life and the power in you. The purpose of your life is referred to as **the birth path** by Kabbalarians (people who practice the Kabbalic system of numerology).

The purpose revealed by your birth path contains the qualities embedded in you, which you have to develop through thinking. It also contains the success you are to achieve and the ideals you need to accomplish. Your personality trait, which is a combination of your strengths and limitations, is also revealed by your date of birth.

Your Birthdate Reveals Your Natural Talents

Generally, your date of birth is referred to as your Life **Path Number**. This number reveals your natural talents. There are abilities you get by learning, but there are some that are inherent. You may not discover these abilities until you are in a position to use them. Sometimes, you discover them when you are under pressure to perform.

However, you don't have to wait until you are under pressure to discover your natural talents. You can know your natural talents by knowing your Life Path Number. Every Life Path number has its own peculiarities. Once you know your Life Path Number and your natural talents, you will simply look for opportunities to show the world what you can do.

When you have a career that is in consonance with your natural talents, your job will become fun. You will not be under unnecessary duress to perform because you are only expressing yourself. Many people struggle to cope with work today because they are in a career that does not give them the ability to express their natural talents. Imagine Lionel Messi is a motivational speaker; he most likely will not be able to achieve the same fame he has by playing football. Hence, you need to know your natural abilities by knowing your Life Path Number.

Numerology Birthday Meaning Calculator

There are various sites that can help you to calculate your Life Path Number. However, you don't need to pay anyone on log on to any site before you can know your Life Path Number. You can calculate it by following a simple procedure. To calculate your Life Path Number, you will add the day of your birth to the month and then the year. For example, if you were born on November 5th, 1992, your Life Path Number will be calculated as follows:

5 + 11 + (1 + 9 + 9 +2)

= 16 + 21

= 37

You will have to reduce the double-digit above to a single-digit number by adding the two numbers together. In other words, you will add the 3 and 7 together, which will give you 10. You will further add the 1 and 0 together, which will give you 1. Hence, the Life Path Number of someone born on November 5th, 1992, is 1. Simple, isn't it? You can try yours now!

What Does Your Birthday Reveal About You?

Now that you know how to calculate your Life Path Number, it is more important that you know the natural talents in store for you according to your Life Path Number. Below are the natural talents you possess as a result of your Life Path Number:

Life Path Number 1

You are result-oriented and a natural leader. You have a strong affinity for autonomy and independence. Your ambitious nature is supported by your discipline and determination to achieve your dream. You are never afraid of obstacles, and you "eat" risk for fun. Your courage and resilience will make others look up to you as a source of inspiration during tough times.

You are incredible, where there is a need to make tough decisions with calmness. You need to watch out for the tendency to always want to box others in and submit to your opinion. That tendency can make you a prima donna who will always struggle with group dynamics.

Life Path Number 2

You are naturally selfless and affectionate. You are tender and caring and always seek to maintain relationships. You are a natural diplomat and willing to make compromises to sustain the healthy atmosphere of any relationship. You need to be careful to avoid letting your emotions always get in the way of your decisions. You will also be an easy target for people who always want to have things go their way even when they are in the wrong. Hence, you need to add some "steal" to your tenderness.

Life Path Number 3

You are creative, optimistic, and love to have fun. Your ability to think out of the box and see what others are not seeing is impressive. Your relentless energy is remarkable and can dissolve negative energy with your burst of life. Your enthusiasm is contagious, and people will always look up to you to lighten up the mood during toxic situations. You need to watch out for being too "playful" when you need to be serious. All play, and no work is not beneficial, and you have to be careful not to get caught in that web.

Life Path Number 4

You find it easy to maintain personal discipline and adhere to a structure. Living healthy is easy for you because you find it easy to obey strict rules like a hygiene regiment. You want to live a simple life, and that can make you almost without any serious ambition. You don't like to take risks, and you need to bring a balance to this tendency. You need to push yourself to take calculated risks once in a while.

Life Path Number 5

You have an unquenchable thirst for freedom. You are adventurous and love to take the risk. You are always on the move, and that makes you struggle with structures.

Your desire for new things is the basis for your unlimited creativity. However, you need to find a structure that works for you because you need a level of discipline to unlock your potentials.

Life Path Number 6

You are responsible and love to nurture and grow things or people. You are a natural teacher who is meticulous in getting your ideas across to people. You are a good link to connect people because of your mediation and reconciliation ability. You also need to pay attention to your own needs. It will be detrimental if you spend the whole of your time meeting the needs of others and totally ignoring yours.

Life Path Number 7

Your imaginative ability is superb, which makes you creative. You are introspective and reflective in your approach to life. You are intuitive and seem to be able to answer difficult questions. However, you need to be careful to be rational sometimes and not always move in the direction of your gut feeling.

Life Path Number 8

You have a strong affinity for power and wealth, and you will get them when you work hard for them. You have it within you to command great influence and affluence. However, you need to be careful not to be too materialistic. You need to avoid sacrificing your relationships for material rewards. You also need to be careful of being too desperate for power. It is not bad to allow someone you believe will do a better job taking the lead instead of you.

Life Path Number 9

You are naturally compassionate and tolerant. You are accommodative and accept people. People will always want to talk to you because you will listen to them and understand them. You have to ensure you are not too trusting and learn from every new experience.

Chapter 6: Reveal the Underlying Meaning Behind the Numbers in your Life

Meanings of Names

The numbers in your life are pointers to the message of the universe to you. Your unique characteristics and journey in life are hidden in there. In this chapter, I will take you through how you can translate your names to numbers. Why? The numbers in your names unveil your personality and capability. You will be able to know whether you are in the best profession for you when you know these numbers.

I will also help you know which lottery numbers you should pick, which increases your chances of success. I will also touch on your lucky phone number and 5 main numbers that can encourage lucky events to happen in your life.

Translating Names to Numbers

When the purpose of a thing is not known, abuse of that thing is only a matter of time. Your names are the "codes" with which the events that come your way in life are written. Your full name as it appears in your birth certificate is your **Expression number.** The vowels in your name reveal your **Soul Urge Number** while your family name reveals the kind of influence your family has on your life. Each of these numbers plays significant roles in your present and future.

Your Expression Number reveals your talent, abilities, weakness, and the likely hurdles you will have to jump in life. This number, as earlier said, is found in your full name as it is written in your birth certificate. How come? Your birth name reveals your personal history prior to the day you were born. Your birth name is not an accident because they are based on the intuition of your parents. This intuition is based on the vibrations created by your guardian angel around your parents.

Hence, when they finally settle on the names, though your parents may not even be aware, they will realize that they have been compelled by an unseen force to go for those names. Therefore, your birth names are the names your guardian angel wants you to have because of the impact of those names on the path you must follow in life to live a happy and fulfilled life.

Your Soul Urge Number reveals your greatest desire. It may sound bizarre because you may feel that you know what you desire the most. However, the shocking truth about life is that most times, you will never know what you desire the most until you find it. Some things you think are the most important to you right now will no longer matter when you find what truly matters the most to you. It is good to know that you don't have to wait until you find that thing before you know that is what you desire the most. So many people die without ever finding out what their soul desires the most.

Thankfully, the knowledge of numerology ensures that you don't have to wait before you know what matters to you the most. All you need to do is to find your Soul Urge number, and there you are! How? Just translate the vowels in your name to a single-digit number, and you will know your Soul Urge number. How can you do that? It is simple. The first thing you need to know is the value of each letter in your name. Below are the values of each alphabet in your name:

A, J, S = 1

B, K, T = 2

C, L, U = 3

D, M, V = 4

E, N, W = 5

F, O, X = 6

G, P, Y = 7

H, Q, Z = 8

I, R = 9

Therefore, if your full name as seen in your birth certificate is Abraham Quiroz Jorginho, your Expression Number will be calculated as follows:

Abraham = 1 + 2 + 9 + 1 + 8 + 1 + 4 = 26

Quiroz = 8 + 3 + 9 + 9 + 6 + 8 = 43

Jorginho = 1 + 6 + 9 + 7 + 9 + 5 + 8 + 6 = 51

After the initial addition of each name, you will then proceed by adding the three double-digit numbers you have obtained together as follows:

26 + 43 + 51 = 120

You will not stop until you obtain a single-digit number. Hence, you will reduce the number to a single-digit number as follows:

1 + 2 + 0 = 3

Hence, from the above calculations, Abraham Quiroz Jorginho's Expression Number is 3.

The Soul Urge Number of Abraham Quiroz Jorginho will be calculated as follows:

AAA + UIO + OIO (Vowels in the names) = (1 + 1 +1) + (3 + 9 +6) + (6 + 9 + 6)

= 3 + 18 + 21

= 42

To obtain the single-digit number, you will add the 4 and 2 together which will be equal to 6. Hence, Abraham Quiroz Jorginho's Soul Number is 6.

Discover If You Are In Your Best Profession Or Focus of Education

It is good to know your Expression Number as well as your Soul Urge Number. However, it is pointless to know how to calculate these numbers if you don't know how to interpret the meaning of the number. Hence, it is important that I help you with the interpretation of any Expression number you have. This understanding of the interpretation of your Expression Number will help you discover if you are in your Best profession or focus of an education.

Below are the interpretations of each Expression Number in Numerology:

Expression Number 1

This number is a leadership number. It shows that you have a natural flair for setting goals and maintaining the necessary discipline to achieve it. You are courageous and not afraid to take a calculated risk. You are ambitious and always see yourself at the very top of whatever you do. You are not cut out for being just a member of a team but as a protagonist. You are the poster boy of your organization and the energy that drives others to achieve the goals and objectives of the organization.

Your front-runner nature makes you an excellent entrepreneur. This number is also for religious leaders, elite politicians, activists, self-made millionaires, and inventors. However, you have to be careful of selfishness and pride. Your confidence in your ability is rooftop, and it may make you count the contribution of others as insignificant. You have the tendency to feel that you don't need anyone to succeed in your life. Hence, you are prone to dispensing people quickly and lacking the patience to help others grow at their own pace.

As a 1, you need to watch out for these weaknesses and maximize your strength. You must never forget that people are not the same. Help people around you grow, and they will never forget the positive impact you made in their lives. If you can successfully do that, you will definitely be at the forefront of great moves and business empires.

Expression Number 2

As a Number 2, you have the natural ability to make friends and connect with people. Most times, it is not because you are trying to be friends with people, but your likable and amiable qualities will draw many people to you. You have an open heart, and you are accommodative of people. You have empathy, and your compassion level is unusually high. You are quick to make compromises to "allow peace to reign." People with Expression Number 1, in particular, will like you to be their friends and partners because you are not confrontational.

Your diplomatic ability makes you more like "the power behind the throne" rather than "being the one on the throne." Therefore, your ability is better suited for being a business partner rather than a business owner. You will be a valuable member of a board in an organization. You will be that link that connects everyone together and massage the ego of individualistic people to create a perfectly working group dynamic.

You will not thrive as much as you can if you are handed a leadership role. You will be diplomatic enough to carry anyone along, but you will not be able to make tough decisions without being too emotional. Hence, you have to learn to value yourself in your position as a supporting cast. No one can do what you do better than you. Hence, instead of envying leaders, rather appreciate your rare quality of being an awesome follower.

Expression Number 3

As a Number 3, you are outgoing, inspiring, creative, and positive. Your creativity makes you a perfect fit for a career in art. You are a social person who has so much positive energy around you. You can inspire people and make them go all out to turn their lives around without trying so hard. You have the natural ability to motivate people and turn toxic moments into positive ones with a snap of your finger. People will like to be around you, and you will have to learn to deal with this.

You will find it easy to attract the opposite sex, but you have to be careful to learn to define your relationships. Failure to handle the attraction of people to you will make you an unfaithful friend and partner because you will be trying to please every person that comes around you. Your natural ability to inspire people will be of good use as a motivational speaker. However, you may struggle to discipline yourself to concentrate on a particular objective for a long time. If you can cope with distraction and focus on your goals in life, you will definitely be a success.

Expression Number 4

Expression Number 4 is the number of discipline and structure. You are not flamboyant and thrive in obeying rules and regulations. You cannot cope when there is no particular instruction you have to follow to attain success. You don't want to be given the license to be "creative." You will be a successful accountant, government official, manager, or accountant. You will also be a good fit for a career in the military where obedience to instructions is the key to success.

You can still venture into a career in music and arts, but your touch of discipline and structure will still be evident. In your relationship with people, you have the tendency to be moralistic, which many will interpret as being a perfectionist. You may struggle to attract many people and will most likely have few friends. You will not be compatible with people who are outgoing. Only people who are disciplined or want to be disciplined will want to come around you.

You have to be careful because of your tendency to be a workaholic who will barely have any time for fun. Your serious approach to life will earn you many plaudits from your superiors, but you have to enjoy the reward of your hard labor too.

Expression Number 5

As a number 5, stability is not your strength. You are ad-free as a bird and love adventure, fun, and anything exciting. Revolting against structures is a norm for you. You will not only crave and fight for your own freedom all through your life but also that of others. You will be very vocal in your criticism of anyone or structure that restricts people from expressing themselves to the fullest. You will not be able to thrive in a setting where there are set rules to be followed, which inhibit creativity.

You need to be careful because your desire for freedom of expression can land you into trouble. You are prone to becoming a drug addict or any other unhealthy practices. Your ability to communicate will make you a good lawyer, politician, sales representative, or public relations officer. Your enthusiasm is infectious, and you will be able to convince people to buy into your idea easily. However, you need to watch out for yourself to maintain enough self-control in every sphere of your life.

Expression Number 6

Number 6 is the number of selflessness and genuine affection for others. If your Expression Number is 6, you are always more concerned about the need of others above yourself. You have a knack for developing a trustworthy relationship with others. Your friends can always count on you because of your honesty and faithfulness. You will easily stand out among other employees in your company as regards integrity. Justice matters to you, and you are never happy to see others suffering, especially for your actions.

You are very creative, but you may struggle to express your ability because you tend to have more time for others than for yourself. Hence, the time you have to develop your ability personally is limited. You are adept at reconciling people and psychological healing wounds. Hence, you will be at home if you have a career in psychology, counseling, and teaching. You will also do well as a farmer, florist, artist, designer, or gardener.

A career in business is not also out of place for you, especially in areas where human relations are very vital. You have to ensure you maintain a balance between the time you spend on helping others and cultivating your own abilities to thrive.

Expression Number 7

7 is the number of truth, knowledge, and analysis. If your Expression Number is 7, your desire for knowledge will be insatiable. Critical life issues that many consider as mysterious will be your focus. You will want to be the one people can look up to for answers to difficult questions. Your analytical skill is excellent, and your ability for logical reasoning is difficult to match. You have the tendency to

keep your thoughts to yourself until you are convinced that the time is right for you to tell others.

A career in science or philosophy will be perfect for you. You will thrive as an analyst, researcher, inventor, lawyer, priest, or banker. Your love for mysticism and investigation will also come in handy as a detective. You have to watch out for too much of keeping your thoughts to yourself. You may find it difficult to connect with people because they will find you too mysterious and secretive. People will feel you are unpredictable, and it can affect your interpersonal relationship because you will be classified as an undependable person.

Your depth of knowledge will also paint you as someone who is too critical of others. Hence, learn to take out time to reflect on your actions. Dismiss falsehood but let it be clear to people that you are attacking their wrong assertions and not their personality.

Expression Number 8

People who have Expression number 8 are designed for the pinnacle of their career. They are fiercely competitive and have the discipline and focus on becoming the very best in whatever they do. Influence and affluence are within their domain. They are great achievers who can break and set records for fun. They will face great challenges, but they are equipped to surmount every challenge and come out tops. The challenges they face will only make them realize their immeasurable potential to succeed.

They are easy choices for leadership positions. A career as an entrepreneur is perfect for such people. They are business owners and have the ability to create a business dynasty that has global coverage. Their focus and discipline make them impossible to stop from attaining their goals. They set the standard for others to follow. However, they have to be careful not to be self-conceited and intolerant of others. Their ability to be focused and achieve their goals can make them treat others as irrelevant.

Expression Number 9

This is the number of humanitarian services, compassion, and idealism. If you have this number as your Expression Number, you have a global view of the world. You want everyone in the world to see themselves as the same and not see any race as inferior. You have the intention to change the world and make it a better place. You have your greatest moment of satisfaction whenever you do something that affects others. A career in law, politics, teaching, or medicine will be a perfect fit for you. Your desire to light up others and alleviate their pain will be needed there.

Prejudice does not have any place with you. You project a cool and loving image to people, and that will draw many people to you. However, you usually don't express what you feel. You believe strongly in the good of humanity, but you are poor in judging the character of people.

Know Your Lucky Mobile Number

On 31st of October 2016, a post on *Bangkok Post* was written on "Extremely Lucky phone numbers could fetch B100 million". According to this post, there were four companies that expressed an interest in bidding for these 16 lucky phone numbers. Why will companies be ready to path away with their hard-earned money for "fun"? Hence, it shows that some mobile numbers actually attract luck to the owners.

According to the post, the 16 phone numbers include 099- 999- 9999, 088- 888- 8888, 090- 000- 0000, 091- 111- 1111, 092- 222- 2222, 093- 333- 3333, 094- 444- 4444, 095- 555- 555, 096- 666- 6666, 097- 777- 7777, 098- 888- 8888, 061- 111- 1111, 062- 222- 2222, 063- 333- 3333, 064- 444- 4444, and 065- 555- 5555.

These companies want to purchase these numbers because they are both easy to remember and bring luck to the owners. The reason for the ability of these numbers to bring luck is primarily because these numbers have a semblance with Chinese names for prosperity and other good things of life. Besides, the sequence of these numbers shows a conglomeration of particular numbers. The positive energies of the conglomeration of a particular number will attract good tidings to the owners of these numbers.

Hence, when choosing a mobile number, consider a phone number that has a particular number being repeated. Such phone numbers will improve the rate at which you have lucky events come your way. When it comes to numerology, as much as nothing is set in stone, you also cannot afford to take anything for granted. A little tweak of numbers can change your experience in life. If things are not working and you are not ready to try something new, you are not doing yourself any good.

Hence, always look out for means of improving your general approach in life, but don't forget to look out for the numbers too. You may be doing exactly what you need to succeed but just have unlucky numbers in your life. It will now look as though you are not working hard enough like your peers; meanwhile, the issue is that you have not had favorable events come your way.

Five Main Numbers that can Encourage Lucky Events to Happen in your Life

Finding lucky numbers in your life is not just real; it is also fun. Every number in the numerological perspective has both positive and negative attributes. However, there are some particular numbers that can encourage lucky events to happen in your life. These numbers will help you with which lottery numbers you should choose.

The first number you should consider is your **Life Path Number**. I have discussed how to calculate it in the previous chapter. It is derived from your date of birth. This number resonates with you and will bring you luck. You can also go with a traditionally lucky number like 7, 3, or 4. Alex Bellos, a mathematician, ran a poll to discover the most popular lucky number in the world. The result of the poll showed that number 7 is the most popular lucky number in the world.

It is not too surprising because the number 7 is quite significant. There are 7 days of the week, 7 continents, 7 seas and other interesting, fun facts. Good things also come in threes and fours. However, you need to be careful about using traditional numbers because there will be many other people using them. Hence, in case you win a jackpot, you are likely to split it. If you have kids, you can also consider the date of birth of your kids.

NB: Never forget that these numbers only gives you a higher chance of winning and not absolute. Any number can make you win a lottery. Hence, don't bet money you cannot afford to lose because you are placing money on a lucky number. That will not be too wise of you.

Chapter 7: Guidance Regarding Property

Every location on earth has peculiar characteristics that make people decide to live there. For some people, they prefer environments where there are a lot of people so that they can have more than enough social interactions daily. For others, they cannot afford to have "noisy neighbors." For such people, even if they don't have enough money to live in such residential areas, it is their dream to live there someday.

It is normal for you to consider various factors such as the safety of your life and properties, economic activities of the location, and proximity to your place of work. However, those factors are not enough bases for your choice of location. You can actually take advantage of your knowledge of numerology when choosing the location of your home or business. In this chapter, I will be taking you through how you can make your life better by choosing your address with numerology in mind.

When Choosing a New Home, should one use Numerology?

Yes. Why? In numerology, numbers are everything. Just like your birth date, your address has numbers associated with it. Never forget that every number in numerology has both positive and negative attributes. Hence, the address of your home or company has both positive and negative attributes that will affect your experiences. Therefore, you cannot afford to sideline numerology when making your choice as regards the address of your home or business.

If you have just moved to a new home, it is important you find out the Home Number of your new address. Knowing this number will help you know what to expect and prepare for future events. You will also be able to make quality decisions as regards staying in that address or leaving the place for somewhere better.

The first thing you need to do know the personality of your home is to know the Number of your home. When I say, "Number of your home," I am not talking about the address of your home but the numerological number of your home. This number reveals the peculiar character and energy of your home. It is not difficult to know this number. The only issue you may have is that there are particular cases in which the number you will focus on will be different. Once you can master the rule for each case, you are good to go.

You need to disassemble and add your address together to know this number. For instance, if your address is at "798 Main Street", you will take out the numbers and add them together as follows:

7 + 9 + 8 = 24

If you get a double-digit, you will have to reduce it to a single-digit further to unveil the unique character and energy of your home as follows:

2 + 4 = 6

From the above calculation, the numerological representation of your home is 6. Easy, isn't it? You can try yours right now. It is fun! However, you may seemingly encounter a challenge if the name of your street is number. I mean, if your address is something like "560 6th Avenue".

You will be tempted to add the number 6 in the 6th to the 560, but that will not be correct. If your address is in this form, you will ignore the name of the street. I mean, you will only add the numbers together as follows:

5 + 6 + 0 = 11

Just like the last example, you will further reduce the double-digit to a single-digit number by adding the numbers together as follows:

1 + 1 = 2

That means your Home Number is 2 in such instance. If you live in an apartment, the method will be a little bit different again. The difference is that the focus is not the same. However, the technique of addition and reduction of double-digit to obtain a single-digit is still the same. You will have to use your unit number in case of an apartment. Your unit number is a unique number for your space.

In case your address is something like "1700 Harry Court, Apt 45", you will ignore the "1700" in front of the apartment address. You will only concentrate on the "45" at the end of the address because that is your unit number. The addition of the two numbers will be equal to 9. It is possible that your address is a little different from the three scenarios that have been addressed so far. It is possible that your apartment or street number contains a letter. I mean, if your street or apartment number is something like "876B,".

In such a situation where there is a letter attached to your street or apartment number, don't ignore the letter! Any Home Number you obtain through the elimination of the letter in such a situation is inaccurate. Before adding the numbers together, you will have to obtain the number equivalent of the letter in the Pythagorean System of Numerology. The number equivalent of letter B in this system is 2.

Note: The full representation of letters with their respective numbers can be found in chapter 6 of this book.

Therefore, if your address is 876B Willow Avenue, your Home Number will be calculated as follows:

8 + 7 + 6 + 2 = 23

Further reduction of the number will lead to the addition of 2 and 3, which will be equal to 5. Hence, your Home number, in that case, will be 5. As have seen, knowing your Home number is not difficult. The only reason why it may seem complicated in some instances is when you don't know the exact rule that applies to the addition of numbers.

How The Address of Your Home Affects You

Now that you know how to obtain your Home Number, it is important to know the implication of your own Home Number. As earlier said, every number has its own peculiar energy and characteristic. Below are the characteristics of each Home Number from 1 to 9.

Home Number 1

1 stand for strength, innovation, and independence. The number one Home Number is perfect for single people or entrepreneurs. This Home Number supports their need for independence, personal freedom, and autonomy. The

energy this number oozes supports the desire to explore and break new grounds. If you are about to or just began a new business, you need to consider an address with this number.

1 feeds you with the energy for the requisite self-confidence to channel your resources in the right direction. Hence, if you desire a life partner anytime soon, you have to desist from living in an address whose Home Number is 1. The energy of this address is all about you and will even affect your chances of starting or maintaining a healthy relationship.

If you have a family already and you are living in this address, you need to consider relocation as fast as possible. The energy of this address does not support the soft and interdependence nature of a family. You don't have to cause trouble in your home by pushing so hard for relocation without carrying others along, especially your partner. Let him or she knows that the happiness of the family is the driving force behind your insistence on relocation.

Home Number 2

A family person leaving an address with Home Number 1 will find an address with Home Number two, a perfect place to grow and nurture a family. The energy of 2 supports building a home to give every member of the family a sense of belonging. If there is an address that is the complete opposite of 1, it is 2. The major difference between two and 1 is that 2 is meant for interpersonal relationships where group dynamics supersedes individualism.

The energy of 2 is perfect for loving relationships and harmonious living. Young families, romantic partners, and roommates who have cordial relationships will enjoy a Home Number 2 address. They will be comfortable there because the energy of the home supports sentiments and sensitivity, which are backbones of cordial relationships.

However, just like every number in numerology, 2 has its negative impacts too. The fact that the energy it oozes supports a family and group structure makes it detrimental to people who thrive on creativity and individual brilliance. If you want to focus on creating a business or single and not interested in building a family anytime soon, 3 is not a good address for you.

Home Number 3

3 is the hub of entertainment and creativity. If you are into a career where the premium is placed on creativity, this is the best home for you. The vibrations of this home provide the much-needed platform for expression and creation of new things. Hence, if you are an artist or involved in a career where expressing yourself in a new and dynamic way is paramount, the energy of 3 suits you perfectly.

3 is also cut out for social gatherings and squeezing as much fun as possible out of life. Hence, if you are the kind of person who likes having interesting people come around you regularly for parties and great times, 3 is your best bet. However, you need to be careful because this number can move you closer to bankruptcy. With much fun and entertainment comes the desire to spend lavishly on liabilities.

Hence, if you have a plan to live a serene life devoid of distraction and extravagance, 3 is not healthy for you. Hence, before you make the decision to live in a Home Number 3 address, you need to decide what matters to you between having maximum fun and living a shrewd, sober life.

Home Number 4

Home Number 4 is the center of discipline and responsibility. Just as 1 is the opposite of 2, 3 is the opposite of 4. The vibration of 4 supports living a discipline, grounded, and responsible life. It does not support fun and extravagance. 4 is perfect for people who want to raise responsible kids and steadily grow their business. The abundance of energy for structure and discipline makes this home a "taboo" for people who love to have a lot of friends come around them often for entertainment.

Therefore, you are adventurous and like to be a little "wild," you will be making a mistake by choosing to live in 5. The energy of 5 supports a stable structure, which is also beneficial if you want to have a home garden. For a low key life where growth and stability are at the top of your list, let an address whose Home Number is 4 be non-negotiable for you. You will struggle to find your feet, and your life will be like that of a fish on the dry ground if you live in 3.

Home Number 5

Just like 3, 5 is a vibrant house for social life. If you have a knack for inviting people to come to your house and have nice times, 5 is suitable for you. The energy of this number resonates with social activities and entertainment. Unlike

3, it does not ooze out the energy for creativity as such but for variety and change. However, the fact that this house promotes variety and instability can be a problem for you. You may find it difficult to live in that house for long.

When you live in this house, circumstances around you will make you want to leave the house and go elsewhere. Hence, if you are looking for a place you can stay for a long time in harmony with your family and proximity to your workplace, 5 is not an ideal home for you. Apart from the vibrant social life, 5 also has the added advantage of making you bold and fearless. The energy of this home gives you the confidence to handle tough situations and come out a winner.

Therefore, you can be sure that by the time you decide to leave the house, you would have learned a lot of lessons in life. 5 is a perfect house to train yourself to be strong and courageous in life to face difficult tasks. Hence, 5 is a perfect stopover for single people before they move on to stability with a family in a Home Number 2 house.

Home Number 6

Home number 6 is similar to Home Number 6 because they both support harmonious living for families. In numerology, 6 is the number that supports homeliness and family setting the most. The energy of 6 makes people feel welcome and at home. Not only you and your family will feel welcome in this home, your guests, too, will feel welcome here. In fact, your pets will enjoy the atmosphere of the home. It is just the perfect sanctuary for a settled, peaceful, and warm setting of love and harmony.

To appreciate the nature of the home, decorate it with nice pictures and comfortable furniture. Flowers and a home garden will also be perfect for this home. Of course, living in a home-like this is not good, for you want to embrace a single life for the time being. The energy will be detrimental to your desire to be independent and enjoy your freedom.

In this home, you will find yourself wanting, and circumstances around you will arrange themselves to get you engaged. You will have to keep running away from "settling down" if you live in a home-like this. Hence, if you are not ready for the responsibility that comes with the stability and interdependence of having a family, 6 is not a good home for you.

Home Number 7

7 is a sanctuary for a quiet, spiritual, and sober life. If you are the kind of person who wants your home to be a haven to stay away from the "noisy world," 7 is your perfect "hideout." The energy of this home inspires deep thought and reflection and can be somewhat secretive. If you are not the kind of person who thrives on simplicity in your approach to life, you will be living in the wrong home if you find yourself in this home.

You will have to simplify your goals and ambition in life, or else, the energy of this home will feel "choking" for you. You will have to remove any clutter from your thought and environment to be able to live in this home without any issue. You need to connect with the energy of this home to feel at home here. 7 is the perfect home for writers or scientists because of their need to have a clear mind for optimum performance.

The energy of this home ensures that you will be able to know yourself as you reflect on your past actions. It will help you make clear, concrete plans about the future and prepare to be a better person in the future. Meditation is a free flow because of the vibration of Home Number 7.

Home Number 8

8 is quite popular because of its energy for prosperity and abundance. The energy of this home supports growth and ambition, which is necessary for success in business. Hence, an entrepreneur or people who have the drive to reach the pinnacles of their career will find 8 a perfect home for them. Hence, if it is very crucial for you to increase your status in life and attain financial independence, this is your best bet.

8 supports growth, and even growth in family size comes with ease here. However, the energy of 8 for growth is not without its detriment. It does not support stability and relaxation; it is all about the increase and upward movement. Therefore, 8 is not a good choice for you if it is more important for you that you have a stable and relaxed atmosphere in your home. The upward movement of 8 brings with it a raucous atmosphere that is not healthy for a happy and harmonious home.

A simple rule of numerology is that you can't eat your cake and have it. You will have to choose the characteristics that are top of your list before you decide which home is best for you.

Home Number 9

The last but not the least is Home Number 9. This is the number of acceptance, compassion, and reality. The energy of this number attracts everyone in the world. In another world, this number does not permit discrimination among people of different races and languages. It is an accommodative number, also called the "International number." The vibe around this home promotes selflessness, forgiveness, spirituality, and creativity.

If you have a global view of making the world a better place through selfless sacrifices and humanitarian services, 9 is the best home for you. The energy this home ooze will help you learn a lot about yourself, and you are inspired to live a life that will leave an indelible mark on human history. If you live in this home, you have to be accommodative and tolerant of being in tandem with the vibration of this home.

Your heart should be opened to all, not for the fun of having people come around you but to make a meaningful impact in the lives of people. People will see you as a source of inspiration and a great example to humanity when you resonate with the energy of this home.

Chapter 8: Having a Perfect Relationship with the Knowledge of Numerology

As you would have noticed by now, the knowledge of numerology can help you in every aspect of your life. In this chapter, I will be narrowing down on the application of the knowledge of numerology to your marital relationship. Well, a perfect relationship is not a relationship where there are no issues. A perfect relationship is a relationship where the couples understand themselves and are willing to make compromises for the sake of the relationship. I don't want you to switch off or flip the pages over because you are already in a relationship. This is because this chapter is not only for people who are single but also for people who are either engaged or married already. You can use the knowledge of numerology to make your relationship healthier.

Hence, read through, and I am sure you will learn one or two things that will make your relationship more worthwhile. If you feel your relationship is healthy, it can even be better with this numerology tips. You can never know the full potential of your relationship until you are exposed to some new experiences. I am convinced that your experience in your relationship will even be far better than it was before you read this book.

Single but Searching

If you are single but interested in hooking up with a good partner, your knowledge of numerology can guide your steps. The most important thing is to find someone who is romantically compatible with you. I don't think I need to preach a sermon to you on the importance of compatibility in a relationship. You may claim to be in love with a person initially, but if you are not compatible with the person, the relationship will fizzle out.

So many people who end up breaking up a relationship had felt they were in love at one point but ended up breaking up the relationship. Hence, if you have plans to fall in love and "stay in love," you need to build a relationship on the right foundation. You cannot afford to build your relationship on only physical attraction because it won't stand the test of time. Physical attraction will bring you together initially, but what sustains a relationship is friendship.

Meanwhile, friendship in a relationship is not possible in the absence of compatibility. You and your partner must complement yourselves to avoid having issues that will be classified as "irreconcilable" in the future. I am sure that you don't want to experience the heartache of breaking up with someone you had taught would be your Mr. or Mrs. Right later. Hence, it is always better to start on the right note.

Starting on the right note means that you have to consider the compatibility of you and the person before allowing your emotions to run wide. The best way to do this is to find your **Expression or Psyche number**. Your Psyche Number can be derived from your birth date. It is gotten from the addition of the day, month, and year of your birth. Check chapter five for a better explanation of the importance of your birth date and how to calculate it.

Romantic Compatibility for Searching Singles

Once you know your Psyche Number, you will have a better understanding of your own capabilities and deficiencies. The resultant effect of this knowledge is that you will be able to know people whose Psyche Number is compatible with yours when it comes to a marital relationship. You will have to know the Psyche Number of the person you intend to date also before you can know whether or not the person is compatible with you.

Number 1

If your Psyche Number is 1, you have a kind and disciplined personality. You have an air of authority and can be arrogant. Hence, a person with Psyche Number 2, 3, and 9 are the best for you. A person with Psyche Number 2 is okay with being given instructions. Such people are submissive and will not have serious issues with being bossed around by Number 1s. A person with Psyche Number 3 will be a loyal friend and likes to teach others.

The loyalty and patience of Number 3s make them perfect partners for a Number 1. They will help Number 1 make better decisions in all facets of life. Number 9s are also ideal partners for Number 1s because they offer valuable partnership and friendship. Their positive energy levels will compensate for the tendency of a Number 1 to be rude and abrasive. If you are a Number 1, and you go ahead to date another Number 1, there will be "two captains in a boat." Two number of 1s dating themselves will soon annoy themselves and break up eventually because of their tendency to be bossy.

Number 2

If your Psyche Number is 2, your best chance of building a solid and lasting relationship is with a 1, 3, or another Number 2. A number 1 will support you and be a "pillar" for your soft, tender, and loving nature. A Number will be glad that you don't lord things over him or her and will, in response, offer you maximum support. A Number 3 will reciprocate your friendship, and you will connect on a philosophical level. Another Number 2 will also suit you because your characteristics are alike. Unlike in the case of two Number 1s, two Number 2s are romantically compatible.

Number 3

As a Number 3, you are friendly, spiritual, hard-working, and independent. You are ambitious, just like number 1s, and that is an important connection. You are more practical than Number 1s, and that will make you capable of helping them execute their ideas practically. Your discipline and focus, just like Number 1s, will make you compatible with them. You will also be compatible with a Number 2.

Though they are not as ambitious as 3, their quality support will make them a good business or life partner for you. Your relationship with a Number 9 will also be productive. The organization skills and industry of a Number 9 will attract you, which makes both of you compatible.

Number 4

If you are a Number 4, your rebellious and secretive nature makes you compatible with a number 2 or 8. A number 5 will offer you good friends, but he or she will not be a life partner. Your secrets will be safe with a Number 5, but you can never be sure of what he or she is thinking, and this unpredictability will not be healthy for you. A Number 2 will be a good option for you because of their calm and tender personality.

The calm nature of a Number 2 will be a perfect foil for your turbulent nature. Just like Number 2, Number 8 is also calm and peaceful, and that will make them good partners for Number 4s. 8s can help 4s channel their extreme energies to something positive, thereby making both of them compatible for a marital relationship.

Number 5

As a Number 5, you have an intellectual and entertaining personality. The mental strength of 1s will make them good business partners and friends but not marriage partners. The restlessness of a 5 makes them good friends to 4s, but they will be hindrances to themselves when it comes to a marital relationship. Number 6s are the best life partners for Number 5s. 6s will help 5s get rid of their restlessness because of their loving and caring nature.

Number 6

6s are diplomatic and polite, and you will be forgiven to assume that they will be good partners for 1s. However, that is not the case because their tendency to be slow will not make 1s happy. 4s, 5s, and 8s are ideal life partners for 6s. 4s restlessness will not be an issue for 6s because they will be there to make them calm and channel their energy positively. 4s are similar to 5s in terms of their turbulent nature, and that will make them good options for 6s as well.

8s will make good life partners for 6s because of their calm and spiritual nature. The tendency of 6s to be too social will also be controlled by the calm and intelligent approach of 8s.

Number 7

7s are inventive and intuitive. They are often unrealistic and mystical in their approach to life. The discipline of 1s and the practical approach of 9s to life make 1s and 9s good life partners for 7s. 2s will also be good life partners for 7s, but they will be financial disasters if they partner in business. Both 2s and 7s are not active and disciplined enough to make quality business decisions. The intellectual capability of 7 makes them attractive to and compatible with 8s.

Number 8

If you are a number 8, you should consider dating a 1 or 2. Your hardworking, intellectual, and visionary personality will appeal to a 1. Though both 8s and 1s are egoistic, the positive energy of 8s is a welcome "disinfectant" for the often negative energy of 1s. The supporting cast personality of 2s makes them good life partners for 8s. However, an 8 may feel a 2 is not industrious enough for him or her.

Number 9

Number 9s are realistic, disciplined, and mentally tough. However, they have short tempers and tend to discriminate against people. Their discipline and mental strength will make them good partners for 1s both in business and marital relationships. The realism of 9s also makes them beneficial to number 7s who can be stuck in their own dream world. Both 5s and 9s will generate good positive energy together, which makes them also compatible.

What You Need For A Healthy Relationship

For vain and materialistic people, the answer to a healthy relationship is dating a rich guy or lady. Well, building a healthy relationship goes beyond the financial capabilities of the two parties involved. After reading through the compatibility for singles through numerology, you may feel you are in a relationship. However, you don't have to break your relationship because of the incompatibility of your Psyche Number.

The truth is that you will have issues abound, but no issues are irreconcilable. Never forget that even if you are in a relationship with someone whose Psyche Number is compatible with yours, there will still be issues that both of you will have to learn to solve and grow together. Therefore, being in a relationship with someone whose Psyche Number resonates with yours does not guarantee anything. It only means that you have a higher chance of building a strong and healthy relationship together.

Therefore, people who are in a relationship with someone whose Psyche Number correlates have a lot of work to do to make the relationship work. If they are not careful, they will find out that people who are not compatible based on their natural attributes will have more successful relationships than them. Hence, as much as it is important to be in a relationship with someone who is compatible with you based on your Psyche Number, understanding the person is more important.

If you are with a 1 who has the natural tendency to be dominating and bossy, if you are a 1 or 8, it can be frustrating. However, since you know that is the kind of person you have, you need to focus more on his or her strength. His or her discipline, focus, and determination to achieve his or her dream should catch your attention. If you learn to value your partner's strength and downplay or overlook his or her deficiency, you are set for a long-lasting relationship.

Even if you are a 1 dating a 2, you will like the fact that he or she is tender and supports you but may not be happy with the level of discipline or ambition of the person. Hence, it should matter more to you that you appreciate the part of your partner you like and be willing to help him or her gets rid of the bad attributes. You may want an easy fix, such as suggesting a change of name to your partner to tweak some of his or her attributes. However, you may successfully get rid of a particular attribute you don't like, but be sure that you will see the manifestation of another negative attribute.

Hence, it is always better you know your partner very well and be willing to help him, or her grow. Love the person unconditionally and be ready to forgive any shortcoming. A healthy relationship is built on genuine affection and understanding. Love does not mean that you will ignore the deficiencies; it means that you will be willing to help the person maximize his or her strength and grow out of his or her defects.

The rate of divorce in the modern world is alarming. A major reason for this high rate of divorce is because people are too quick to change relationships. A lot of people have very unrealistic expectations of relationships. No one is perfect. A long-lasting relationship is a deliberate choice to focus on what your partner can do and overlook what he or she cannot do.

Know Your Lucky Date of Marriage

The last part of this chapter is how you can pick a lucky date of marriage. After you have picked a life partner who is compatible with you, you will have to fix a date for your marriage. As a believer in numerology, you should not be frivolous about the date you pick for your marriage. The date you pick will play a role in the fortune of your marriage in the future. Hence, it is always better to be deliberate about your choice.

Your choice of date of marriage should be based on your Lucky Number. Your Lucky Number is your Life Path Number, and it is a derivative of your birth date. Once you find out your Lucky Number, you are good to go. Pick a date that resonates with your Lucky Number to attract a better future for you and your spouse. Your marriage is the beginning of a new life, which promises a lot of possibilities.

Marriage is not a bed of roses, and you have to be mentally ready for it. There will be challenges to navigate and a lot of pleasant moments too. Choosing a wedding date that is in consonance is a good way to start this new life with your partner. You can explain your reason for picking that date to your partner in case of any objection. Dialogue is important in marriage to build a lasting relationship. Hence, if you let your partner be aware of your faith in the power of numbers from the onset, he or she will not term it as unnecessary superstition later on.

However, if you feel your partner is not matured enough or ready for the information, you need not bother him or her for now. You can wait until when you are convinced that he or she can handle the information correctly before explaining how the number influences our experiences as humans on earth. A successful marriage is not impossible or too difficult. The only issue is that many people are not willing to pay the price to get it right.

Chapter 9: Establish Your Business Based On Your Lucky Number

The joy of every businessman or woman is to make a profit. However, making a profit in business is not automatic; you need to be deliberate about it. In other words, you need to take practical steps to ensure that you succeed in business. I don't need to bore you with general principles such as getting your products and services across to the right market or creating a plausible business strategy. You probably know all these before now.

However, if you don't, it is important you understand general foundational business techniques before you invest your money. I know you are eager to know how you can establish your business based on your lucky number. However, I need to be sincere with you here. The knowledge of numerology does not **automatically** mean that you will succeed in any sphere of life, including business. What the knowledge of the power of numbers does for you is to give you an edge in life.

Some believers in numerology are now either pessimists or critics. Why? Their perception of the edge numerology gives people in life was wrong. They expected numerology to take care of the basic aspects of their lives that were meant to be their responsibility. Hence, they felt disappointed and lost hope in the ability of the numbers in their lives to help them live a happy and fulfilled life.

Numerology helps you channel your energy and resources in the right direction. Hence, in this chapter, as I take you through how you can establish your business based on your lucky number, have it in mind that you also need to put in the hard work. This knowledge will make your chances of success higher and not an automatic ticket to becoming successful in your business.

Numerology to the Rescue!

You need to be confident in your chances of becoming a success in your business. Hence, as you start your new business, remove every apprehension or anxiety from your mind, and tell yourself you will succeed. It is okay to be a little bit anxious because you are investing a lot of time, effort, energy, and finance into the business, and you don't want it all to be in vain. However, it is a problem when anxiety begins to impair your performance.

You need not be afraid; numerology has answers to help you become a money magnet. I am sure you are happy to hear that. All that you need to succeed has been deposited in you by the Universe already. Within your core numbers lies the secret of your success. Hence, the knowledge numerology comes in handy to help you marshal your business towards unprecedented success and progress. Financial independence is not elusive for people who are able to walk within the confines of the path the universe has laid down for them.

First things First

The first thing you need to do to establish your business based on your Lucky Number is to find out the number. You don't need a fortune-telling expert to help you with that. If you have been paying attention so far, you should know by now that your Lucky Number is your Life Path Number. Your Life Path number is derived by adding all the values attached to the alphabets in your name together, which will give you a double-digit number. Reduce the double-digit number to a single-digit number by adding the two digits together. There you go!

Now that you know your Lucky Number, you are ready to select the appropriate business name for your new business. In the world of numerology, you cannot afford to take anything for granted. Your business name has to resonate with your lucky number to give you an edge to succeed in your business. In other words, your business name goes a long way in determining whether you will succeed or not. Fortune or stagnation in your business can be altered by simply tweaking the business name to the one that is in alignment with your Lucky Number.

If you already have a business name and have started the business already, it is not too late. If you find out that your business is not yielding as much profit as your hard work deserves, you need to do something fast. I believe what matters to you is the profit and not the name of the business. Hence, if a business name is not helping you realize your potential in business, a little or major tweak to it to maximize profit is a no-brainer. You don't need to convince anyone about the reason for your actions as long as it is the right action.

It is normal that there will be people who will criticize you because they don't understand you, but you need to stand your ground and do what you must do. Hence, when it comes to both minor and major decisions in your life that will turn your life around positively, you need to be more concerned about how the decision affects you. The end justifies the means, after all. Hence, if you are convinced changing your business name will change your fortune in the right direction, why not?

Why does it Matter?

Any right-thinking person must have a reasonable reason for his or her actions. I don't mean that the reason has to be reasonable to others; at least, it has to be reasonable to the person. Hence, it is important that I give you tangible reasons why you need to establish your business based on your Lucky Number. You may think that the reason is obvious because your Lucky Number will help you attract the right people for business, which will, in turn, lead to more profit. However, it goes beyond mere attracting the right people or attracting the right deals.

When you find out your Life Path Number, you will be able to know your strengths and weaknesses. This discovery is particularly important and beneficial if you are yet to start a business. Hence, before you even think about a business name, you would have known the career path that is best for your abilities. In other words, you will know the best business that maximizes your strength and can cope with your deficiencies.

Your life Path Number will also help you determine the kind of people you will have in your business team. You will only recruit people who can be cooperative and supporting such that they will be able to help you achieve your objective. You may not be able to apply this rule to everyone you employ in your company. However, you have to be careful about the people you have in your inner circle. Hence, for such people, you should be concerned about their Life Path Numbers so that you will not have people who will rebel against you or betray you.

Should I be an Entrepreneur or Employee?

Knowing your Life Path number will unveil to you whether you are better off working for others or starting up your own business in the first place. It sounds ridiculous in the modern world today, where almost everyone wants to be a business mogul or tycoon who owns several business chains. It is a good ambition, and anyone who achieves that will be glad. However, it is one thing to dream; it is one thing to have the capacity to achieve the dream.

For example, people who have number 1 as their life path number have leadership qualities such as a strong determination, independence, creativity, and boldness that makes them better entrepreneurs. They can pioneer a business successfully, especially when they are able to reduce the impact of their weaknesses, which include impatience and selfishness. Hence, if your Life Path Number is 1, you are good to go as regards becoming a business owner.

People whose Life Path Number is 2 are cooperative, warm, and diplomatic. They can be entrepreneurs too because of their people skills, but they are better team players. Their attributes are best suited in a business sense when they are part of a company's board. They will always ensure that they don't allow their sentiments get in the way of the objectives of the company. Besides, their tendency to have low self-esteem will be masked when they are not the ones calling the shots. Hence, if your Lucky Number is 2, it will be better if you find someone or people with a vision and mission for a business that resonates with them and helps them succeed. Your invaluable contribution in itself is a success for you.

It is better to be a successful "supporting cast" than become a disaster while playing the leading role. The problem is that most people are not realistic. No one can succeed alone. Every great people in this world, whether in business or another sphere of life were able to succeed because of people who were willing to be at the background of their success. The world is designed in such a way that we cannot all be a protagonist. Some people have to lead while others support them.

Any leader without quality support will crumble. Hence, those in the leading role must be humble enough to acknowledge the effort of those willing to sacrifice for them to succeed. In the same way, those playing the supporting roles must be happy to do it without envying the leader. Why some famous business dynasty crumbled is because they had people who were not happy with their roles who wanted to take the place of the leaders.

True success in life is living a happy and fulfilled life and not necessarily being in the Forbes list. Fame and wealth are good and must be desired. However, the key to living a happy and meaningful life is living life, knowing that you are doing something that offers you the opportunity for maximum expression of your capabilities. If owning a business allows you to maximize your strength and diminish your weaknesses, why not? However, if being part of a successful business team offers you maximum expression, don't be desperate about leading a business team.

I am not in any way discouraging you from achieving your dream of owning business chains (if you have such ambition), I am only more concerned about your happiness because that is what matters the most. Besides, you are still somewhat a business owner if you buy shares from a company because that makes you a stakeholder in the company. Therefore, you have a part to play in the decision making of the company. Hence, your path to fame and wealth is not limited to being a pioneer of a business. You can grow your money via investment in a working business model and still smile at the bank.

Life Path Number 1 Only?

It is important to know that I am not saying that the only people that can succeed as business owners are people whose Life Path Number is 1. I will not be accurate to make such an assertion because it is not true. People with Life Path Number 4 will also make good leaders because of their affinity for orderliness. They are steady, self-disciplined, logical, and orderly. These attributes are essential in leadership. However, they will have to watch out for their tendency to be perfectionists and too demanding.

People with Life Path Number are visionary and resourceful, which are good for leadership, but their tendency to be disorganized, irresponsible, and unstable is not good for business owners. 6, just like 2, is also a better team player rather than a leader. People with this Life Path Number are compassionate and responsible. People with Life Path Number 8 have the best attributes for business. They are ambitious, courageous, and influential. They have all the necessary ingredients to succeed as business owners even above people with Life Path Number 1.

However, they have to be careful to avoid being greedy and materialistic. They have the tendency to sacrifice the happiness of others for their own selfish gain. They also need to be careful about arrogance and the tendency to want to control others. These attributes of Life Path

Number 8 inspires a lot of people to change their names or business names such that it will resonate with this number. Such people have to be careful because they cannot accept the positives that come with the Life Path Number 8 and totally reject the negative attributes associated with it.

Best Business Based on Lucky Numbers

Since your Life Path Number reveals your positive and negative attributes, it also helps you know the best business for you. You will struggle if you choose a career path that does not maximize your strength and diminish your defects, you will feel like a fish on dry land; you will be out of sorts. For example, if your Life Path Number is 3, you will thrive more in a business that allows you to be creative and display your magical use of words.

Hence, a career in creative and verbal art will be better for you. Within your core attributes is a good sense of humor. Hence, a career as a public speaker or acting will suit you the most. Your tendency to talk too much will not be obvious in such careers because you are paid to talk after all. Hence, no one will notice your defect, unlike when you find yourself in a career that demands temperance and orderliness.

If your Life Path Number is 4, your affinity for orderliness and discipline will make you thrive in a career like the military. Your resilience and perseverance will come in handy in a career like that, and your inability to fit in perfectly in a social setting will not be obvious. If your life Path Number is 6, a medically-related career will suit you. Your natural ability to care and nurture people will stand out in a career like that. The nature of the work is predictable and can be boring, but it suits you well. It would have been a disadvantage elsewhere, but you will be at home in a career like that.

You will be at home in a career where knowledge, analytical skill, and a studious nature are important if your Life Path Number is 7. Your natural ability to also be inventive will make you thrive in engineering or other careers where technological advancement very vital. Your tendency to be withdrawn and calculative will rather be seen as a strength rather than weaknesses in such careers.

Hence, you need to know your Life Path Number so that you will be able to follow a career path that suits your abilities. Even if you want to change your name to get attributes for a different career, it all begins by knowing your Life Path Number in the first place.

The Best Business Strategy Based on Lucky Numbers

If you are convinced that your path in life is to be a business owner based on your Life Path Number, then it is right for me to help you with picking the best name for your business. If you are into a partnership, you also need to convince your partner to know his or her Life Path Number so that both of you can make the necessary alterations in your names together. It is important both of you make the changes together because your fortune is not enough to determine the fate of a business that is not owned by you alone.

Your business partner does not only contribute his or her money to the business; he or she also contributes to his or her luck. After changing the names as necessary, you are ready for the name of the business. If it is a running business, register the Partnership Deed on your lucky day based on your lucky number. Your brand name should also be changed to reflect your lucky number. Just like I have said earlier, you cannot afford to take anything for granted. Every little detail of your business can affect the success of the business. Hence, pay attention to every detail.

You should also look at your meeting days. As much as it is within your power, ensure you have your business meetings on days that resonate with your lucky number. For your brand color, too, go for colors whose names resonate with your lucky number. It may sound ridiculous, but a detail such as brand color, which you may want to underrate, goes a long way in determining the kind of deals you attract.

Hence, your best business strategy in the numerological sense is to establish your business based on your Lucky Number. This may sound basic, but you must be intelligent with the way you tweak the name of your company or brand name. If your business deals in agricultural products, you cannot tweak the name such that it reflects something related to tech or the medical field. The message you want your products and services to pass across to your clients is what matters first.

You cannot afford to confuse your prospective clients because you want your business name to reflect your Lucky Number. Hence, determine the message first before you determine the best name for your company and products. I have said earlier that you need more than luck to succeed in business. Luck only gives you an edge and not the ultimate thing. Hence, you have to be intelligent with the way you go about tweaking your name, your brand name, or company name.

Such mistakes will make you doubt the effectiveness of numerology when you don't achieve the desired result. Hence, the practice of numerology is not for people who cannot think. You have to be deliberate, strategic, positive, and logical to succeed as a businessman or woman who understands the power of numbers.

Chapter 10: In popular Culture

In this chapter, I will take you through some movies and film shows where numerology featured predominantly. Various topics and themes are used in various popular television and films. Ideas such as serial killers or Zombies are common. However, there are also quite a number of movies, and film shows where numerology was either a central or partial theme. In these movies and film shows, the main idea was to show to the audience how people are using the knowledge of numerology to live a meaningful and fulfilled life.

The influence of the media can be positive or negative. When it comes to numerology, the media has dissuaded many people from taking the power of numbers to offer explanations about important questions of life serious. However, thanks to the media, many people have become more interested in finding out the veracity of the claims of numerology. An example of such a positive influence of the media in fostering the knowledge of numerology is the "Davinci Code." The Davinci code made a lot of people become interested in finding out more about practices that have deeper implications in life.

I must confess that in some movies, numerology was not accurately presented. Hence, you will be making a big mistake if you think you already know what numerology is all about because of what you saw in a movie or TV show. However, the intentions of the writers and directors were right. They were able to display that numerology is not an archaic science that has no practical application in the modern world.

These movies and film shows were able to prove that the lives of people can have deeper meanings through the exploration of the knowledge of the magical power of numbers, thereby starring more people to consider numerology as a science that offers tangible answers to some of life's most important questions. I will bore you or overwhelm you if I pick every movie, novel, and film show where numerology was either a central or partial theme. Hence, I have only selected a few that are some of the best around.

The Davinci Code

The Davinci Code is a movie produced based on a book that was written with the same title by Dan Brown in 2003. This movie was produced in 2006, and it really did a lot of good to the awakening of people to the power of numbers. The core themes of the movie include mysticism, spirituality, religion, and the fight for power. The Fibonacci Sequence is one of the most popular number sequences in the world. In Davinci Code, the Fibonacci Sequence was hidden in an interesting way. The Fibonacci Sequence is a number series such that the value of the next number is equal to the sum of the preceding numbers.

The Fibonacci Sequence is approximately the number of the Golden Spiral. The Golden Spiral is found in the universe and in nature in your ear, snail shells, and in pine cones. In the Davinci Code movie, the Fibonacci Sequence was used in a simple but powerful way to unlock a safe. Amidst the thrill, suspense, and drama of the movie, the power of number unfolds dynamically and a major take away from the movie.

In the movie, a professor of religious symbology, Robert Langdon, is the suspect in the murder of Jacques Sauniere. The police found a cipher on the body and began their investigation to fish out the murderer. The investigations lead them to solicit the help of Sir Leigh Teabing, a notable British Historian. Sir Leigh informs the Police that the real Holy Grail can be found in the painting of Leonardo Davinci, The Last Supper. A secret cabal within the Opus Dei was also searching for the true grail to prevent the destruction of Christianity.

The movie and the book were criticized by the Roman Catholic Church as an attack on Christianity. Nonetheless, both the book and the movie went viral. The movie was the second highest-grossing movie in 2006.

Touch TV series

Touch is an American 2-season series produced in 2012. This TV series starring Kiefer Sutherland was originally aired on Fox and was created by Tim Kring. In this series, Sutherland, who played as Martin Bohm, had an interesting relationship with his son, Jake, who was played by David Mazouz. Martin lost his wife during the September 11 attacks in the World Trade Center and had to raise their 11-year old son, Jake alone. Jake was diagnosed with autism, and Martin had a torrid time raising him. He had to move from one job to the other because of the special needs of taking care of his son.

In the movie, Jake does not speak but has a strong affinity for numbers and patterns relating to numbers. He often spends a lot of his time writing them down on his touch-screen tablet or on a notebook or even popcorn kernels. Jake's fascination with numbers gave him the unusual ability to see the "pain of the universe," according to Professor Teller (Danny Glover). Martin realized that his son had been communicating with his with numbers all these while.

He began to follow the leading of his son through numbers and started achieving more positive results in his daily activities. His devotion to Jake was affecting his social service and scrutiny of his ability to retain the custody of his son. Martin saw the gift of his son as an opportunity to make life more meaningful for others and was using it to help people. However, there were corporations (Aster Corps) who had other plans for the gift of Jake. They killed Professor Teller and were trying to lay hold of Jake by forcing the state to relinquish Martin's custody rights.

Touch was short, but the message is clear: there are awesome possibilities to have a better experience as humans through the power of numbers. It was evident from the movie that the universe is communicating with us through numbers. Those who are able to take advantage of this communication have a higher chance of living a happy and fulfilled life. These communications may be through other people, animals, or a spiritual medium.

VALIS

VALIS is a little old because it was written as far back as 1981. Nonetheless, it is one of the best Novels in terms of investigating the power of numbers. VALIS is a science-fiction novel written by American writer Philip K. Dick. The full meaning of VALIS is a Vast Active Living Intelligence System. VALIS is a Gnostic vision of a single aspect of God, according to Dick. The novel is the first of three series of novels, which was never completed owing to the death of the author. It is an interesting novel in which the writer presents his life as one of the characters of the Novel.

According to Dick, there is a transfer of information from an extraterrestrial species and humans via "pink laser beams." The extraterrestrial species use "disinhibiting stimuli" to communicate to humans via symbols, which activate recollection of intrinsic memory. Dick claimed that he was able to recover his son from the claws of death through his alignment with the message from VALIS. He cited that doctors got the diagnosis of his son wrong, but he insisted they carry out another test in which they diagnose his son of inguinal hernia, which could have killed the child if not quickly operated.

In the story, Horselover Fat was convinced that his visions hold the key to understanding the realities of life on earth. Interestingly, the meaning of "Philip" in Greek is "Fond of horses." Also, the German word for "fat" is "dick." Other researchers who shared similar views with him joined him on his journey to investigate the veracity of these matters. VALIS and the Davinci Code have something in common: the use of the Fibonacci Sequence. The Fibonacci Sequence was used in VALIS as the identification signs of a group of people called the "Friends of God."

Number 23

This movie is a psychological thriller starring Jim Carey, albeit in a non-comedic role. It was written by Fernley Philips and directed by Joel Schumacher. In this movie, he was obsessed with a particular novel he believes was written about him. The book was presented to him as a birthday gift by his wife, Agatha (Virginia Madsen). He noticed that there were a lot of strange similarities between the main character of the Novel, Fingerling, and himself.

Jim Carey's character in the movie, Walter Sparrow, believed that the number 23 is deeply connected to his life and will help him have a deeper understanding of his life. This movie featured a glimpse of the number 23 enigma. The number 23 enigma is the belief that every event has a connection to the number 23 or its derivative via permutation. Walter warned his wife about this number, but he didn't make any sense to her, and she told him he was crazy.

He read in the book that Fingerlings murdered his girlfriend, and he started having dreams related to him killing his wife. Walter was referred to Isaac French (Danny Huston), Agatha's friend, who suggested that he should find the author of the book to find the answers he craves. In the movie, the number kept popping up everywhere, both directly and indirectly. It can appear in the form of seeing a staircase with 23 steps or searching for something in room 23 of a hotel.

Sometimes, the number is derived through the use of a simple code by the character in which every letter of the alphabet is numbered from 1 to 26. In that order, a name like "Ned" will equal 23 (14 + 5 + 4). Another important point in the movie was when the main character read every 23rd word in the novel, which helped him locate an address that helps him put the pieces of his lost memory together.

Pi (II)

This movie is the story of a number theorist. The obsession of Max, the protagonist in the movie, to unlock the secret of nature makes him engage in extreme self-destructive behaviors. Max is an unreliable narrator as he suffers from hallucinations and paranoia. He is convinced that numbers explain everything and finds it difficult to make any sense of the patterns in the systems around you.

In the movie, he came across a number, a 216 sequence that seems to make a bold financial prediction. It was initially rejected bur came true. Various lead to the work of Max gaining the attention of a Hassidic group and a Wall Street firm. The Wall Street firm was interested in the financial implication of the number while the Hassidic group believes the number will usher in the messianic age for them. What followed was a paranoid and tense chase causing Max hallucinations and terrible visions that ultimately lead to the loss of all the knowledge of everything Max was trying to find out initially.

There are three main themes in the movie: Kabbalah, the game of go, and mathematics. The Kabbalic theme is seen in how that Pi unveiled the concept of the "Explicit Name." The manipulation of the number 216 letter word will generate 72 columns of the three-letter names of the Hebrew God. The mathematical theme is seen in how Max was able to find a golden spiral showing up wherever he looks. Max believed that any phenomenon could be explained by understanding the mathematics that embodies the golden spiral. The golden spiral is a shape that has been of interest to great scientists, including Pythagoras and Roger Penrose. The growth of the shape is based on the golden ratio.

The game of Go is an ancient game dated as far back as over 2,500 years ago. The complexity that arises from the simple set of rules of the game has always inspired the study of mathematics. In the movie, the characters used the game as a model for their perspective of the universe. They believe that the game is more of a microcosm of the chaotic nature of the world around them.

Numb3rs

Numb3rs TV show reflects the positive role of numerology in the lives of people. This crime drama had six seasons that have the mathematical genius of an FBI agent's brother in focus. The FBI agent's brother uses his mathematical ability to help his brother solve crimes. Every episode of Numb3rs ends in such a way that the FBI agent will end up solving a crime with the aid of the mathematical ingenuity of his brother.

Numb3rs is not without its flaws. For example, it often features unrealistic and questionable mathematical concepts primarily because of the way the script of the drama was written. It is almost as though the plots have been written completely beforehand in such a way that spaces were left for the insertion of mathematical terms that will appeal to the audience before filming, just like the scripts of Star Trek.

Hence, sometimes, there is no link between the mathematical term and the events. However, despite this shortcoming, the characters were able to successfully display how a person can go about the pursuit of the knowledge of numerology personally. Numerology was often portrayed in the film show as a knowledge that can help people have foresight about future events that will unravel in the future. The Gemetria, which is an alphanumeric code of giving words or phrases numerical value based on its letters, was also in extensive use in Numb3rs.

Numerology and Gemetria were used as viable tools for understanding the world around us in the film show. In Numb3rs, the characters were able to pay attention to the patterns in the numerical relationships around them. This awareness of numerical patterns, which helps us to unlock knowledge that was previously hidden, is a major part of numerology. Without any form of mysticism, those who are skillful in numerology will be able to identify these numerical links.

Bee Season

This movie was adapted from a book whose title is also called "Bee Season." It is an American drama in which the daughter of a perpetually dysfunctional family displayed an unexpected knack for winning spelling bees. This newfound success disrupted the dynamic of this family as members of the family begin to discover themselves and have a spiritual awakening as the girl inch closer to winning the national competition.

Numerology is not the major theme in this movie but a part of the lives of the characters who were husband and wife. The husband, played by Richard Gere, is a professor of religious studies who wrote a graduate thesis on the Kaballah. Meanwhile, the wife, played by Juliette Binoche, converted to Judaism after their marriage. She was living a secret life based on her belief in the "tikkun Olam," which is a Kabbalistic belief that humans have a shared responsibility in transforming and repairing the world. "Tikkun Olam" is a Jewish word that means "repairing the world."

Her husband took a special interest in her after realizing that she had inspired her with his own spiritual beliefs. Hence, he began to coach her by employing his Kabbalah techniques. This new interest leads him to pay a lot of attention to his wife at the expense of the children. The key lesson from this movie is how a person can utilize the Kabbalah in everyday living. Though numerology did not play the major part in the plot of the movie, it was a deliberate insight into how a lot of people are using the knowledge of numerology to have a better experience in their lives.

11-11-11

11-11-11 is a horror film written and directed by Darren Lynn Bousman in 2011. It has the number 11 written all over it from the storyline to the release date. It was set at 11:11 on the 11th day in the 11th month and released on November 11, 2011. In the movie, Joseph Crone, a writer, played by Timothy Gibbs dreamt that his wife and son were trapped in their burning home and eventually died. He woke up by 11:11 in his hotel room on November 7, 2011.

Joseph was involved in a car accident on November 8, 2011, that got him hospitalized. His MRI scan showed that he was not hurt, but the driver had died. When he checked his wristwatch, it was 11:11. His brother, Samuel (Michael Landes), called him that night to inform him that their father (Denis Rafter) was dying. Joseph went to see his father the next day in Barcelona, where his brother showed him a security video called "de los demonios." The video showed a faint outline of a demon at 11:11 pm.

Joseph informed Samuel about how he had seen 11-11 frequently recently. Ana, the local housekeeper, informs Joseph based on a diary titled El Libro de Ana, which is the gospel according to her that the number sequence shows that Joseph has been "Activated." Joseph rescued Samuel that night from creatures looking like demons who were trying to strangle Samuel. Joseph later finds a photo in the custody of Javier who had tried to kill Samuel with the words "SACRIFICIO" scribbled on it.

Joseph was convinced that Samuel is a prophet that the demons were trying to kill so that the "Serpent" will rise and birth a new religion after the destruction of the church. However, he was wrong as he found out too late that Samuel was actually the devil that he should have stopped. The movie ends with time in the future when a large congregation was reading a book titled "The Book of Joseph."

Other Worthwhile Mentions

Other works on numerology worth mentioning include XKCD and Harry Potter. XKCD is a famous internet comic serious written by Randall Monroe. Randall Monroe is a former NASA roboticist. This internet sensation that touched on math, science, love, and philosophy made the best use of the Fibonacci Sequence. In Harry Potter, Numerology was practiced in the name of **Arithmancy,** which was an elective course in "Harry Potter and the Prisoner of Azkaban."

FAQ

There are many questions people ask about numerology out of curiosity or pessimism. It is quite difficult for some people to believe that understanding the properties of numbers in their lives can be enough to answer questions about life. Below are frequently asked questions about numerology and the answers:

Is numerology all about mathematics?

For those who do not like mathematics, you don't need to be afraid because numerology is not all about mathematics. Numerology is the science of numbers, and there are aspects where you have to do a mathematical operation like a simple addition when finding your core numbers. Numerology is all about understanding the attributes of numbers and how they affect your life. You don't need to obtain a degree in mathematics before you can successfully understand and practice numerology. Numerology is a deliberate exploration and answer to difficult life questions like your purpose and greatest drive.

Can numerology predict my future?

The answer to this question is "No" because it is not God. However, numerology can help you understand the reasons for the events unraveling themselves in your life. Therefore, numerology can help you know the kind of events that are likely to take place in your life in the future. However, your understanding of the numbers in your life does not automatically mean you will achieve success or fail in the future. The course of your life is determined by the actions you take or did not take.

Are there good and evil numbers?

People who do not understand the properties of numbers in numerology often assume that there are numbers that are inherently positive or negative. However, it is not true that there are numbers that have only positive or negative attributes. In numerology, every number has both positive and negative properties. Hence, before you are hell-bent on changing your name to alter some characteristics or events in your life, you need to think twice. You will have to accept the positive attributes of your core numbers and do your best to limit the negative attributes so that you can have balance in your life.

Is there is a connection between numerology and religion?

No. Numerology is not a religion but a universal science. Numerology is not only about human beings but can even be applicable in the case of animals. Both humans and animals have the date they were born. Hence, numerology helps us understand the positive and negative attributes of both people and animals. In other words, your name or the name you call your pet has both positive and negative attributes in numerology. Numerology is the knowledge of the energy of the vibration energies of numbers and not a religion.

What kind of answers does numerology answer?

Numerology helps you to understand who you are, your path in life, your motivation, and your direction. Questions about your personality, strengths, and weaknesses are all answered through the knowledge of numerology. Numerology can help you know your natural talents and the best career path that suits your characteristics. You can also know the right person to marry, the kind of business you can invest, and the kind of location that is best for you. You can know when you need to be patient and when you need to make changes in your life through the knowledge of numerology.

Can I know my soul mate through the knowledge of numerology?

Yes! You can know whether your current relationship is the right one through the knowledge of numerology. Your Life Path Number reveals your purpose, strength, and weakness. Hence, you can determine whether you are romantically compatible with a person or not when you know the Life Path Number of the person. You can know whether the person's strength complements your weaknesses and vice versa. Hence, numerology can help you know who to avoid and who you should give a chance to win your heart and stay in your life.

What is the difference between numerology and astrology?

Astrology deals with the movement of planetary bodies and their effects on our lives. Astrology is quite rigid and unchangeable because you cannot alter the movement of planetary bodies. However, in numerology, you can alter the events in your life by altering your name. At its peak, astrology is like a mirror. You can see yourself and your features, but you can do nothing but to accept the image presented to you by the mirror. However, numerology is like plastic surgery. If there are aspects of your life you are not comfortable with, you can make alterations in numerology to have new experiences.

Is numerology all about my date of birth?

Numerology is not concerned about your date of birth alone. It is easy to think numerology will only utilize your date of birth because it contains numbers. However, your birth name and the name people call you are also of importance in numerology. Your full name can be converted to digits through the addition of values that are assigned to the letters that make up your name.

Is Nameology the same as Numerology?

"Nameology" is a part of a whole while numerology is the whole. Nameology is the analysis of name vibrations based on values in numerology. Numerology helps you to understand how the numbers in your name affect your life both positively and negatively.

What is the importance of my name in numerology?

Your name determines the positive and negative experiences you will have in life. Therefore, your name plays a very important role in numerology. When people change their names because of unfortunate reasons such as a divorce, it is a big deal in numerology. When the name is converted to a digit in numerology, the attributes of the old and new name is not likely to be the same. Hence, your name says a lot about you in a numerological context. Hence, you have to be careful before you change your name because it may change your fortune.

Conclusion

What a journey! I am convinced that every doubt and question you have about numerology should have been resolved by now. It is okay to have your doubts about numerology because you are an intelligent person. Intelligent people don't just accept whatever they are told until they have verified it for themselves. There is lots of propaganda and false things appearing or claiming to be true out there. Hence, it is normal for you to want to be double sure before you believe in the veracity of numerology. Your desire to find out things for yourself must have convinced you to purchase this book in the first place.

Unfortunately, some people dismiss numerology without verifying their claims. Such people will never know what they are missing until they somehow change their minds and check out the authenticity of the claims of numerology. I am glad that you made the decision to take a leap of faith to find out if numbers indeed have the answer to important questions of life. I am sure by now that you are happy to have committed your energy and time to read through this book.

Do more than Reading!

It is good that you have read the book, but you should do more than that. You have to practice what you have read. Unfortunately, so many people read books for the sake of amassing more knowledge. Some read wide so that whenever there is an argument, they will be able to contribute without feeling like a fish out of water. However, if you read a book like this and you didn't take it to the next level to practice, it is all futile. You are not better than people who don't believe that numerology is real if you have the knowledge, but don't put it to use.

In fact, pessimists and critics of numerology are better than you if you are not taking advantage of the knowledge of numerology to improve your life. At least, such people will not waste their time and effort on reading something like this. In the long run, you will have the same kind of experiences and uncertainty they have in life in spite of your knowledge. The fact that you are working in a soap industry does not automatically mean you will be clean. You have to take the soap and take your bath with it before you can be clean.

In the same way, reading a book on numerology does not automatically mean you will enjoy the benefits of understanding the magical power of numbers. You have to apply your knowledge to every area of your life before you can enjoy the benefits of having the knowledge of numerology. Nothings come your way on a platter of gold in life; you have to show that you are ready to do what is necessary to make things work before you can succeed in life. You have to be deliberate about changing your life if you truly want to have new positive experiences.

For example, I don't expect that you won't know your core numbers by now! You should have calculated and known your Life Path number, Expression Number, and Soul Urge number by now. The best time you should practice whatever you are learning in life is immediate. When you procrastinate, you will start losing the enthusiasm you had initially when you first received the knowledge. Over time, the knowledge will become stale, and you may even start doubting the veracity and relevance of the knowledge.

If the reason you are yet to practice what you have been learning in this book is that you wanted to wait until you are done, it is okay. It is not too late to make amends. The first thing you need to do is to calculate your core numbers. Once you know your core numbers, find out the meaning of those numbers and how they reveal your identity. Discover your personality and your capabilities. Identify your weaknesses and start working on how you can curb them to live a happy and fulfilled life.

Live a Happy and Fulfilled Life!

The ultimate reason this book was written is to improve your experience in life. In other words, this book was written to help you live a happy and fulfilled life. Therefore, if you know your Life Path Number, Expression Number, Lucky Number, Soul Urge Number, and Destiny number but fail to live a happy and fulfilled life, the objective of this book is not fulfilled. Every chapter of the book was deliberately filled with information that will improve your life.

I have done my best to provide you with accurate information that will make you make the best decisions through your knowledge of numerology. Hence, the ball is in your court. No one else apart from you can decide whether you will live a happy life or not apart from you. Every area of your life can experience a tremendous turnaround if only you want it to be so. You can make the right choice about your career path because you understand your natural talents. You know you're your strengths and weaknesses and the best career that suits your capabilities.

You can make the right choice martially because you now know people who will not be suited for you. Hence, you will not only consider how beautiful or cute a person is; you will look at the person's compatibility with you. You will be able to make the right choices about where you live because you know that your address affects the positive and negative experiences you have.

Hence, it will be a major disaster if you end up not living a happy and fulfilled life in spite of all these "weapons" you have. It will mean that you have chosen not to "fight" when you have all you need to win. I believe you will not let me down; you will make use of the invaluable information you have received. Not doing so is ultimately letting you down.

References

Bullinger E. W. (1921). Number in Scripture. Eyre & Spottiswoode (Bible

Warehouse) Ltd.

Campbell F. (1931). Your Days Are Numbered: A Manual of Numerology for

Everybody. DeVorss & Company. ISBN 0-87-516422-6.

Drayer R.A. (2002). Numerology, The Power in Numbers, A Right & Left Brain

Approach. ISBN 0-9640321-3-9.

Five types of numerology - Patristic Center. (n.d.). Retrieved October 20, 2019,

from http://www.patristiccenter.org/five-types-of-numerology/

Hans, D. (2017). Single-Digit Numbers. Retrieved October 22, 2019, from

https://www.worldnumerology.com/numerology-single-digit-

numbers.htm

Hans, D. (2017). Master Numbers. Retrieved October 19, 2019, from

https://www.worldnumerology.com/numerology-master-numbers.htm

Hans, D. (2017). Karmic Debt Number in Numerology. Retrieved October 24, 2019, from https://www.worldnumerology.com/numerology-karmic-debt.html

Hans, D. (n.d.-c). Numerology Compatibility | Numerology.com. Retrieved October 24, 2019, from https://www.numerology.com/numerology-news/numerology-compatibility-life-path-number

Hans, D. (n.d.-a). Expression Numbers | Numerology.com. Retrieved October 23, 2019, from https://www.numerology.com/numerology-news/expression-number-numerology

Kari, S. (n.d.). Numerology for Your Address – Is Your Home Happy for You? Retrieved October 19, 2019, from https://karisamuels.com/home-numerology/

Milton, B. (2013, March 11). Numerology in popular culture. Retrieved October 23, 2019, from

https://sapientparadox.wordpress.com/2013/03/12/numerology-in-

popular-culture/

Nagy A. M. (2016). Numerology Workbook: using Chaldean Mysticism

(Paperback).

Pochat W. & Pirmaïer M. (2011). The Unveiled Numerology – vol. 1 – You do not

necessarily carry the name you think.

Sara, C. (2018, October 26). Meaning of Life Path Number. Retrieved October 22,

2019, from https://www.refinery29.com/en-us/life-path-number-

numerology-meaning

Schimmel A. (1993). The Mystery of Numbers (a scholarly compendium of the

connotations and associations of numbers in historical cultures). New

York, USA: Oxford University Press. ISBN 0-87-516422-6.

Terry, F. (2016, October 31). "Extremely lucky" phone numbers could fetch B100

million. Retrieved October 21, 2019, from

https://www.bangkokpost.com/learning/advanced/1123520/-extremely-lucky-phone-numbers-could-fetch-b100-million

The Types of Numerology. (n.d.). Retrieved October 16, 2019, from

http://www.spiritlink.com/kinds.html

The Connection Between Numerology And Astrology. (n.d.). Retrieved October 17, 2019, from https://www.astroyogi.com/articles/the-connection-between-numerology-and-astrology.aspx

Thanks for Reading!

What did you think of, **Astrology & Numerology: The Power Of Birthdays, Numbers, Stars & Their Secrets to Success, Wealth, Relationships, Fortune Telling & Happiness Revealed**

I know you could have picked any number of books to read, but you picked this book and for that I am extremely grateful.

I hope that it added at value and quality to your everyday life. If so, it would be really nice if you could share this book with your friends and family by posting to Facebook and Twitter.

If you enjoyed this book and found some benefit in reading this, I'd like to hear from you and hope that you could take some time to post a review. Your feedback and support will help this author to greatly improve his writing craft for future projects and make this book even better.

I want you, the reader, to know that your review is very important and so, if you'd like to leave a review, all you have to do is click here and away you go. I wish you all the best in your future success!

Also check out my other books, just search "Sofia Visconti" in store

Thank you and good luck!

Sofia Visconti 2019

A SPIRITUAL START!

Start your week with gratitude, joy, inspiration, and love.

Healing, motivation, inspiration and guidance straight to your inbox every week!

FIND OUT MORE

www.ingramcontent.com/pod-product-compliance
Lightning Source LLC
Chambersburg PA
CBHW071227080526
44587CB00013BA/1527